4 FORTNITE EXPLAINED
How did Fortnite become so huge, and what's the back story? Your questions are answered!

6 FORTNITE LINGO EXPLAINED
Don't know your whites from your blues? Are you bamboozled by other gamers' speech? Worry not – we explain everything!

12 YOUR INVENTORY EXPLAINED!
How to make sure you carry the right equipment for your gaming style.

16 TICK, TICK...BOOM!
Blowing things up is a big part of Fortnite, and we can help you get more bang for your V-buck.

20 TOP STAR WARS SKINS!
The Force is strong with this one. A look at some of our favourite Star Wars skins available through the Item Shop.

22 HIDE AND SEEK
Sometimes, it's best to lay low and wait for the battle to blow over. Find all the best hiding places with our guide!

26 GAMEPLAY TACTICS
Whichever mode you play, some skills are always essential. Learn from the pros with our guide.

32 SOLO TACTICS
A lone wolf who won't work with a partner? Step this way for an insight into the best solo tactics to employ.

34 DUOS TACTICS
Having a partner means you can employ more advanced battle tactics – we reveal some of the most cunning!

36 TRIOS TACTICS
Proof that three is not a crowd – our comprehensive guide to working together can help you claim the win!

38 SQUADS TACTICS
Teamwork makes the dream work! Find out how you can come out on top of the pile with our guide.

40 TOP SPORTING SKINS!
The Island might not be ready to host the Olympics yet, but it's certainly home to some pretty cool sports skins!

42 TEAM RUMBLE TACTICS
It may seem like a huge melee, but there are things you can do in Team Rumble to make sure you end up on the winning team.

44 FORTNITE
Learn how to play
– whether you're an impostor or not

48 TOP CLASSIC SKINS!
Fortnite does a great line in collabs, but some of our favourite skins are original to the game – here are some of the best.

54 TOP ANIMAL SKINS!
Life on the Island is a zoo at the best of times, so why not suit up in one of these animal skins and go the whole 'hog'?

56 QUICK BUILD GUIDE
How to throw up a structure without even thinking about it – a crucial way to stay safe!

58 ADVANCED BUILDING GUIDE
Once you've mastered the basics, time to move on to some of these builds to give yourself a crucial advantage.

60 BATTLE PASS PROGRESSION
Maxing out your ranking isn't about playing lots – it's about playing smart. Read on for some insider hints on how it's done.

62 GAME SETTINGS EXPLAINED
Making sure your controls are set up to suit the way you play can make a huge difference. We'll explain the best things to tweak.

66 TOP FORTNITE LEGENDS SKINS!
You know a game has really made it big when the people that stream it are famous enough to earn a place in the game! Check out our fave Fortnite legends!

68 TOP ONLINE FORTNITE STARS!
The biggest YouTubers and Twitchers out there, and how following them can keep you one step ahead of the crowd!

72 TOP COLLAB SKINS!
Fortnite is amazing at bringing in characters from other universes. Here are some of our favourite skins that started life elsewhere.

74 STAYING SAFE ONLINE
Fortnite is all about having fun, but to do that, you need to stay safe. Our online safety guide contains tips on how to stay safe online.

76 QUIZ CORNER!
So you think you know Fortnite, eh? Try our fiendish puzzles to show off to your friends and prove your devotion to the game.

78 QUIZ CORNER ANSWERS
Find out how you did in our quizzes. No peeking!

LittleBrother BOOKS

Published 2022.
Little Brother Books, Ground Floor, 23 Southernhay East, Exeter, Devon, EX1 1QL
books@littlebrotherbooks.co.uk | www.littlebrotherbooks.co.uk

Printed in China. Xuantan Temple Industrial Zone, Gulao Town, Heshan, Guangdong.

The Little Brother Books trademarks, logos, email and website addresses and the GamesWarrior logo and imprint are sole and exclusive properties of Little Brother Books Limited.

FORTNITE EXPLAINED

THE STORY

The backstory to Fortnite is, well, crazy and complicated. The team clearly have fun bending the rules of time and space, but at the heart of it is a battle between the Imagined Order and The Seven, two mysterious organisations who have an interest in the Island. Along the way, it's pulled in material from Marvel's Avengers, Star Wars, Alien vs Predator and John Wick. Don't try and keep up – just enjoy the action.

When Fortnite first launched way back in 2017, Epic Games – the people behind the game – had a very clear vision of how the game would work. The focus was on a game mode called 'Save The World', which would see players working together to hold back hordes of monsters. The game featured the ability to build elaborate forces to repel the monsters and to craft new weapons alongside the more traditional third-person shooter elements of the game.

Epic's masterplan was that people would pay for the Save The World mode, and that's how the game would turn a profit. However, while working on the game, Epic's developers began playing an early release version of Player Unknown's Battlegrounds, which featured a Battle Royale mode – where 100 players would eliminate each other until only one was left.

microtransactions in its first three days – further evidence of the game's rapidly growing popularity.

They loved it so much that they began to use Fortnite's engine to build their own version of the game. The two development teams were split, to avoid delays to Save The World, but the plan was still to ask players to pay to have access to both games.

Just two weeks before the game launched, Epic decided to make Battle Royale free-to-play. Their motivation was probably to give people a taste of the game so that they would go on to buy Save The World. They had no idea how successful that miscalculation was.

Battle Royale mode simply exploded. The number of players grew at a rate Epic never predicted, and with YouTubers and Twitch streamers jumping on the bandwagon, a global smash hit was secured. Epic began to put more focus on developing Battle Royale mode, with the focus on microtransactions becoming the new business model. Skins, wraps, back bling and emotes were snapped up eagerly by fans keen to express their own identity.

Ports to other formats followed, with the game racking up over $1 million in

Today, the game has over 350 MILLION registered players, and has peaked with over 15 million online at the same time. It's taken its place in popular culture with celebrities imitating the dance emotes and countless references to it in film and TV shows. In the first half of 2022, around 270 million players played the game each month.

Battle Royale mode may have started as an afterthought, but it has grown to be one of the most popular – and profitable – games of all time. So sit back, enjoy the rest of this annual and know that you are part of one of the biggest gaming communities of all time!

BIRTH OF A LEGEND

The initial default skins were really intended to serve as a blank canvas for those who hadn't splashed out for their own skins yet. However, Jonesy, one of the default skins, has emerged as a central figure in the storyline and is now a legitimate gaming icon in his own right!

FORTNITE LINGO EXPLAINED

WHEN YOU START PLAYING, IT CAN SEEM AS IF EVERYONE ELSE IS SPEAKING A FOREIGN LANGUAGE! FEAR NOT, OUR HANDY GUIDE WILL HAVE YOU SOUNDING LIKE A PRO IN NO TIME!

AFK
Away from keyboard. Used when a player is still in the game, but isn't actually playing. "Let's box her up to protect her, she's AFK."

AR
A shorter way of saying Assault Rifle. "I've got two ARs, does anyone want to take one?"

A Large Shield Potion is usually called a Big Pot

BIG POT
A large Shield Potion, which will restore 50 shield to a player. "There's a big pot on top of that hill."

BLUES
Refers to all healing items that are blue in colour. These mainly repair shields, but some will also repair health. "Has anyone got any blues, I'm low on shield."

BOT
Either a fake player controlled by AI, or a player that is so bad they play LIKE a fake player controlled by AI. "That guy was such a bot!"

BOX UP
The act of building a box with the player in the middle to defend against attack. "They're opening fire, box up quickly!"

CRACKED
Used to tell team-mates that a player has no shield left. "I just hit her with an AR and cracked her!"

CRANKING 90s
The act of building a tower with stairs in quickly, by building at 90 degree turns. "I'm firing at him but he's cranking 90s."

Building a tower under fire is 'cranking 90s'

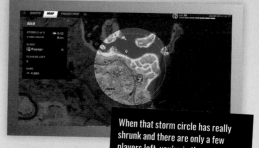
When that storm circle has really shrunk and there are only a few players left, you're in the endgame...

ENDGAME
Used to refer to the last couple of stages of the game, where there are only a handful of players left. "We need to make sure we have lots of mats for the endgame."

FARMING
The process of gathering materials, especially during the early part of the game, to make sure you have plenty in reserve. "Let's get farming while it's nice and quiet."

HEALS
Any item that will repair health or shield. "Is everyone carrying heals?"

HOT DROP
Landing in a location that is full of other players, meaning a battle is inevitable very quickly. "Look out everyone, this is looking like a real hot drop!"

KNOCKED

Used in team games to refer to a player who has had their health and shield reduced to zero and is crawling on the floor, but who has yet to be finished off. "I've knocked the guy near the stairs, make sure the others can't get to him!"

Any materials are referred to as 'mats' as a group.

MATS

Short for materials. "I'm running low on mats; can anyone drop me some wood?"

MINIS

Small shield potions, that will increase a player's shield by 25, up to a maximum of 50. "I've only got 10 shield, anyone got any minis before I take my big pot?"

NERFED

This means a weapon's usefulness has been softened, making it much weaker (as if it was loaded with foam Nerf bullets instead of real ones). "They've nerfed the Tactical Shotgun in the latest update."

OG

Short for 'Original Gangsta' but refers to something that's been in Fortnite from the start. "That guy was wearing an OG skin."

OP

Short for overpowered, suggesting a weapon is just too strong. "The Drum Shotgun is just too OP at the moment."

POI

Point of Interest – specifically, a place on the Island that is given a name, but doesn't show up on the map. "There's a new POI this week; you can gain XP by visiting it"

PUSH

The act of aggressively attacking another player or team's location with the aim of eliminating them. "Let's push now while they are reloading."

RES

Reviving a player who has been knocked. "Someone res me quickly, before they push our location!"

SHOTTY

Short for a shotgun, and refers to the whole branch of weapons rather than anything specific. "Does anyone want to swap my AR for a shotty?"

Anything from the shotgun family is known as a 'shotty'

SPRAY

The act of firing blindly with an SMG or a machine gun, and just hoping that you hit someone. "I can't believe he got me, all he could do was spray."

STRAIGHTLINE

Heading directly to the storm circle, and not deviating for any reason. "Storm's closing in, we need to straightline it if we are going to make it in time."

SUB

No, not a delicious sandwich, but short for 'sub machine gun' or SMG. Again, it refers to the whole class of weapons. "Has anyone got any ammo for a sub, I'm running low?"

SWEAT

A player who tries harder than they need to in order to secure a win (the suggestion being they are trying so hard they break into a sweat). Typically, this includes elaborate building and boxing players in. "That guy was such a sweat, he built around me and set fire to it instead of just shooting me."

TAC

Although lots of weapons are preceded by 'tactical' in Fortnite, this phrase specifically refers to the Tactical Shotgun. "Does anyone want to take that blue tac? If not, I'll have it."

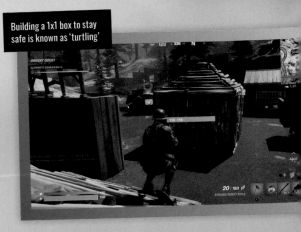
Building a 1x1 box to stay safe is known as 'turtling'

TURTLING

Building yourself a 1x1 box in combat to avoid damage. "I've got her pinned down but she's turtling!"

VAULTED

What happens to weapons that are taken out of the game. They are said to have been 'vaulted' - but that doesn't mean they won't return! "Man, I'm totally gutted that they vaulted the Boogie Bomb."

Weapons can be vaulted or unvaulted – a vaulted weapon is no longer available to use in the game

WHITELINE

The same as 'straightline' - meaning to get straight to the storm circle. "It's a long way to the storm; we need to whiteline it."

Bandages and MedKits are referred to as 'whites'

WHITES

Heals that will impact only your health – usually bandages and MedKits. "I'm badly hurt, does anyone have whites?"

ZONE

The eye of the storm. "Let's go now; we need to get to zone quickly."

HOW TO MASTER NO BUILD MODE

AT THE START OF CHAPTER 3 SEASON 3, EPIC DROPPED A HUGE SURPRISE BY DISABLING BUILDING. IT PROVED SO POPULAR THAT EVEN WHEN BUILDING WAS RE-INTRODUCED, THE NO-BUILD MODE REMAINED AS A PERMANENT ADDITION. HERE'S HOW TO MAKE THE MOST OF IT!

TAKE THE HIGH GROUND

It's important at the best of times, but the fact that you can't build means having the high ground is absolutely essential in No Build Mode. Whenever you are moving, your focus should be immediately on finding higher ground for the journey. If you encounter someone on the way, you need that high ground advantage.

PLAN YOUR ROUTE

If you are running from the storm, you must remember that you can't build if you find your route blocked by a cliff face. Most players are used to building a ramp to get out of trouble, but you no longer have that luxury. Instead, you need to plan your route ahead, and it makes sense to get moving early so you don't find yourself caught in a panic once the storm starts moving!

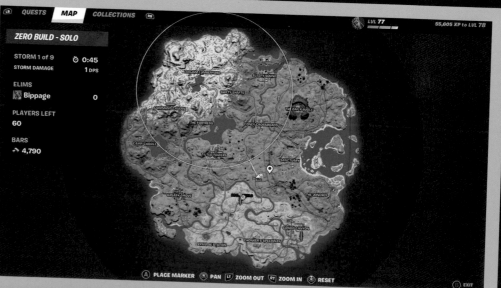

TAKE QUICK HEALS

You can't build to protect yourself while you heal, so look to make the most of quick heals. Choose Chug Splashes over Large Heal Pots, for example, because they are quicker and you won't need to sit still for five seconds to take them. Make the most of any opportunity to boost your health or shield quickly and while moving (the Med Mist is ideal for this).

MOVE IT OR LOSE IT

At the same time that No Build mode was unveiled, Epic introduced some new moves into the game, partly to compensate for the lack of building. Using them is absolutely essential. In particular, the ability to sprint is needed when you have no option other than to cross an open space – it will help you minimise the time you are out in the open. Mantling (dragging yourself up on a surface) is also absolutely crucial as it can help you reach higher areas than you might otherwise have access to. Master the new moves as quickly as you can, and use them every time you play.

USE COVER

Because you can't build a wall to shield you from gunfire, you need to use cover wisely. Stay close to walls and cliffs as you move around the map, and avoid open spaces. If you do come under fire, you'll be close to existing cover within the game which you can use to hide while you figure out where you are being shot from.

ANYONE ORDER AN UBER?

Using vehicles in No Build Mode is another crucial strategy to employ, especially if the storm circle has not been kind to you. They'll help you cover ground while acting as a kind of shield themselves, which will at least give you some kind of warning when you come under fire. What's more, you can use them as cover once you jump out, by crouching behind them (but make sure they don't take so much damage they blow up!).

FIRE IS YOUR FRIEND

Without the ability to build, lots of players are turning to hiding in No Build Mode. Flushing them out can be difficult, especially later on in the game when there is every chance there is someone hiding in the bush you are looking at. By using weapons that spread flames, such as the Firefly Jar, you can destroy cover and force those sneaky campers to reveal their locations. Use that to your advantage.

TEAMWORK MAKES THE DREAM WORK

When playing duos, trios or squads in No Build Mode, it's crucial to work as a team. You can't afford to get separated because a heavy concentration of fire can take a straggler down in seconds. Instead, stay close to each other and make sure you communicate clearly. When you encounter another group of players, you should all focus your fire on one player to get a quick knockdown, then carry on through the team focusing on one at a time.

BLEND IN

Wearing camo gear is more important in No Build Mode than the normal game – anything you can do that keeps other players from spotting you is worth a try. If you are playing as a squad, it's also a good idea to wear the same skin – that way, other teams will find it harder to know who they have already hit and who they haven't.

CHANGE YOUR LOADOUT

You'll probably want to reconsider what you carry in a game when there is no building. Quick heals are worth having, but if you can only find slower heals like Large Shield Potions, you might want to leave them behind and take another weapon instead. It's highly unlikely you'll get enough of a break in combat to make use of the heal, so you'd be better off with a weapon instead.

Similarly, weapons like SMGs that are great for taking down cover are of less value. You'll probably find two shotguns are useful, as a lot of the combat is at close range, and a sniper can be a great way to take opponents out without having to run at their defended position from a long way off.

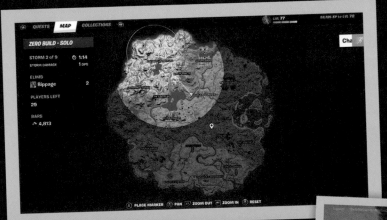

MOVE EARLY AND DEFEND YOUR POSITION

Getting a good position on the field of battle and defending it is key. You want to be in position early, having selected a place with good cover. Moving late and being mobile as the storm circle closes is not recommended, because those players who have already moved into defendable positions will be picking you off for fun. As such, the trick is to try and get central into the zone as quickly as you can, and avoid moving unless you have no alternative.

OVERSHIELD

The Overshield is helpful as it always replenishes. It takes the edge off being sniped from nowhere when you can't build cover, but make the most of the fact that it will recover over time. If someone gets the jump on you and lands a couple of shots, take cover and WAIT. It's tempting to rush straight out and return fire, but you should wait until your Overshield has recovered first. Similarly, if you have landed a couple of shots on someone and they have taken cover, it can be worth pushing hard before their Overshield is back to full strength.

YOUR INVENTORY EXPLAINED!

GETTING YOUR PAYLOAD RIGHT IS A KEY PART OF FORTNITE. EARLY ON IN THE GAME, YOU'LL NEED TO MAKE DO WITH WHATEVER YOU FIND BUT AS YOU SURVIVE INTO THE LATER STAGES, YOU'LL HAVE THE CHANCE TO TAILOR WHAT YOU ARE CARRYING SO THAT IT MATCHES YOUR GAMING STYLE. WE'VE COMPILED A HANDY LIST OF THINGS TO BEAR IN MIND WHEN MANAGING YOUR ARMOURY.

PREFERRED ITEM SLOTS

In a pressure situation, it's crucial that you know your shotgun is next to your SMG, for example. Knowing what is where will quickly become second nature, meaning you don't waste valuable time looking at your inventory to find something – and never again will you suffer the shame of throwing heals at an opponent instead of shooting them.

E   LB 🖥 ⚙ ▤ ⌨🖱 🎮 🔊 🔳 🎮 👤 RB

FERRED ITEM SLOTS

FERRED ITEM SLOTS	<	ON	>
DOUT SLOT 1	<	CONSUMABLE ITEM	>
DOUT SLOT 2	<	SHOTGUN	>
DOUT SLOT 3	<	SMG	>
DOUT SLOT 4	<	ASSAULT RIFLE	>
DOUT SLOT 5	<	UTILITY	>

LOADOUT SLOT 5

Assign a weapon or item type to Slot 5 of your inventory.

A common use for Slot 5: Unassigned.

• Rarity swapping will occur when picking up a higher rarity like-for-like item. Eg. Uncommon Pump Shotgun will swap for an Epic Pump Shotgun. The lower rarity item will be relocated to the first available slot.

• Auto-Sort Consumables to Right will continue to work

• Preferred item slots will only be active until you have a complete loadout.

UNASSIGNED
ASSAULT RIFLE
SHOTGUN
SMG
PISTOL
SNIPER/BOW
LAUNCHER
▶ UTILITY
CONSUMABLE ITEM

PAYLOAD CHOICES

The way you play the game will influence what you should be carrying – here are some popular patterns you might want to follow. Remember that it's better to have the right weapons rather than worry about their rating. It's all well and good having five Epic Shotguns, but you won't have the equipment you need to make it through to the endgame. Get the right weapon in the right slot, then worry about finding an improved version of it!

EXPLOSIVES PAYLOAD

If you like to blow things up and burn your opponents out of their cover, these are great settings to go for.

1) Heals
2) Shotgun
3) Assault Rifle
4) Firelighters
5) Explosives

STANDARD PAYLOAD

This payload will suit most players and caters for a wide variety of scenarios.

1) Heals
2) Shotgun
3) SMG/Assault Rifle with no scope
4) Assault Rifle with scope/Sniper Rifle
5) Explosives/Firelighters

LONG-RANGE PAYLOAD

Like to keep a distance? Then this is the kind of look you want to achieve in your inventory!

1) Heals
2) SMG
3) Assault Rifle with scope
4) Sniper Rifle
5) Explosives/Firelighters

CLOSE RANGE PAYLOAD

These choices will work best if you like to get up close and personal when it comes to combat.

1) Heals
2) Shotgun
3) Another shotgun
4) SMG
5) Assault Rifle

SHOTGUNS

The shotguns are the kings of the close range weapons. They aren't accurate from anything more than a few feet away, but up close they cause a huge amount of damage and can take down opponents in just a couple of shots, even if they have full shields.

The drawback with shotguns is that they take a while to reload and don't have big magazines, so you'll need to take this into consideration. Ideally, look for a shotgun that can fire multiple times without having to be reloaded. The Drum Shotgun is without a doubt the king of the shotguns, but you'll also get good returns from the Auto Shotgun. Others do more damage – such as the Pump Shotgun – but they require reloading so if you miss your opponent, it can be game over!

ASSAULT RIFLE WITH SCOPE

These aren't always available and will often be vaulted – but when they are available, they make a great choice for long-range combat. Yes, they lack the range of a Sniper Rifle but they have a higher fire rate to compensate. If you're packing one of these instead of a Sniper Rifle, avoid extreme long-range combat (over 100 metres, broadly speaking) because they'll do less damage and it's harder to hit an opponent. But for the 'lower end' of ranged combat, they are the superior choice.

ASSAULT RIFLE WITH NO SCOPE

These tend to be Combat Assault Rifles or Ranger Assault Rifles, though other types are available. Again, they aren't always available but they make good medium range alternatives to SMGs – they offer slightly greater range so are useless up close, unlike the SMG which has a foot in both camps. The lack of a scope means they aren't too good for engaging at distance, though they can still do some damage if you have no alternative.

SMGs

SMGs (short for sub machine guns) can be used at close range to cause large amounts of damage thanks to their rapid rate of fire, but they also make reasonable weapons over the mid-range. When used in extreme close quarter battles it can become a bit of a lottery, as you will need to rely more on a 'spray and pray' technique, but with opponents 5-10 meters away, they can quickly eliminate players even with full shields.

Combat SMGs pack more of a punch but you need to watch the kick on them – it's hard to keep them accurate over a prolonged burst of fire. The Stinger SMG is almost as powerful but with a much lower kick, so is the better option if you are considering using an SMG as a mid-range weapon.

EXPLOSIVE ORDINANCE

Examples of explosives would be grenades, plastic explosive or rocket launchers. They are things that cause an explosion rather than fire, and that's how they do their damage. They can serve the same goal as firelighting weaponry, namely to destroy cover but they can also cause direct damage and this is how they are used most effectively.

SNIPER RIFLE

In some seasons, the Sniper Rifle reigned supreme, but as the game has developed, it is of increasingly less value. The drop can be hard to master, especially when you only have a few seconds to take aim and fire. As more and more players are savvy to the threat of the sniper, it's also increasingly rare to find players who stay still long enough to line up a shot properly, so unless you are an absolute expert with the weapon, its usefulness has certainly been diminished. Other variations such as the Heavy Sniper Rifle or the Automatic Sniper Rifle may be available at various times – the latter is probably the most useful variation.

FIRELIGHTING ORDNANCE

One of the biggest gamechangers in Fortnite was the development that allowed buildings to catch fire. That single change made weapons that can spark a fire – such as fireflies and flare guns – much more valuable. Use these to set fire to structures that players are using as cover, forcing them into the open. This might be buildings or their own structures (provided they are made of wood) but works just as well if they are hiding in bushes or in wooded areas.

HEALS

There are different categories of heals, and what you should carry may change over the course of a game. Heals will do one of three things – heal your shield (Shield Potions, for example), heal your health (Medkits) or heal both (Chug Splashes). Early in the game, prioritise heals that will repair your shield, ideally Large Shield Potions or Mini Shield Potions. If you have a long way to travel through the storm, then you might find it better to carry Large Medkits, as the storm will leave your shields as they were but deplete your health.

Later on in the game, it pays to look out for heals that operate QUICKLY. Shield Potions take time to drink, and if you are down to the last few members, taking time out to drink is a luxury you may not have. Instead, look for things like Chug Splashes or even large quantities of food (such as Shield Mushrooms) as they will repair your shield almost instantly, meaning you're less likely to be taken out while trying to heal up.

TICK, TICK...
BOOM!

FORTNITE IS HOME TO A LOT OF EXPLOSIVE WEAPONRY, SO IT'S A GOOD JOB WE'RE HERE TO SHOW YOU HOW TO GET THE BEST OUT OF IT!

GRENADES

They may be one of the simplest forms of explosive weaponry in Fortnite, but they absolutely remain one of the most effective – and they are very rarely vaulted, so it is worth mastering their use.

The trick is realising that they do not detonate on impact, but will bounce first to arm and THEN explode. To make the most of that, aim either at the ground in front of your target or a wall behind them so that they are in the

danger zone when the Grenade explodes. If you are throwing them at an opponent who is turtling frantically, practice your timing so that the first grenade destroys a wall and the second passes into their building in the split second before they can replace it.

Lastly, never throw Grenades uphill. If your opponent is at the top of a hill or a tower, throwing a Grenade at them can backfire horribly if it drops down straight back at you.

CREATING A ROLLING BOMB

Sometimes, you don't have weapons like Grenades or Firefly Jars that will explode on impact, but you can still take out opponents at a distance if you are smart. One way to do this is to use a weapon as a rolling bomb. Stick C4 or a Proximity Mine onto a vehicle, then drive it towards your opponent. Jump out at a safe distance, and watch as the vehicle continues heading towards their position. When it's close enough, hit the detonator and blow them sky high. If you don't have any sticky explosives, you can achieve the same results by rolling a badly damaged vehicle towards your opponent. A few direct hits from your guns should have a similar effect!

ELIMINATIONS WITH FIRE

This is a masterly skill, and one that requires some planning. However, the introduction of fire has changed the dynamic in Fortnite, and makes it easier to take out opponents who are hiding in buildings.

If you have explosives that cause fire, such as Fireflies or a Flare Gun, then you can use them to flush out your opponent right where you want them. The trick is not to aim directly for the building they are in first. Assuming you have three Firefly jars or three Flare Gun shots, try to use the first two to set fire to the ground AROUND the building they are cowering in. Your opponent will think you've made a mistake, and that your aim is off. That's when you hit the third shot on the building they are in. Now, in order to flee the flames, they'll have to run through MORE fire, sustaining more damage as they go!

You can take this plan on a phase, and deliberately leave an area untouched, so you know where they will run in order to escape the fire – somewhere you'll already have your sights focused on!

USING ROCKET LAUNCHERS

Rocket launchers and similar weaponry such as the Anvil are appealing options, but be aware that they aren't foolproof. Both weapons are quite slow to reload, comparatively speaking, and they will usually give your position away thanks to the smoke and light they emit. That makes them useless for covert attacks – the joy of a grenade or Firefly Jar attack is that it is hard for your opponent to figure out exactly where it came from. They also tend to leave you vulnerable to a counter-attack because they are slow to reach their target, giving your opponents the chance to flee before impact and return fire.

While they deliver a lot of damage, it arrives very slowly. Weapons like this are best avoided in solos, because you will likely need a team mate to accompany your attack with gunfire, as well as to keep you safe while reloading.

USING THE ENVIRONMENT

Another way to secure an explosives elimination is to use the environment. This requires seeing the bigger picture, and being willing to think a little out of the box. In a gunfight, it is very easy to focus entirely on your opponent's location and not look at what else is going on around them.

Very often, their surroundings will be as dangerous to them as your bullets are. Look out for flammable objects such as gas cans, exploding cannisters, or good old-fashioned petrol pumps (if you are engaged in a shootout at a gas station). Focusing your fire on explosive items such as these will cause them to ignite, and the subsequent fireball could very likely finish off your opponent. Even if it doesn't, it will result in a fire and then your target has to move, often out into the open where you can pick them off more easily.

LEAVING A BOOBY TRAP

You don't always just have to hope there'll be the chance of hitting a gas can, of course. You can set booby traps yourself, and lie in wait until an opponent blunders into them.

The most obvious example would be rigging an appealing car, such as a whiplash, with C4 and waiting for someone to run along and jump into it before you detonate it. Other devious tactics include hiding C4 in a building or next to petrol pumps, but you can still set up booby traps without an actual explosive. Grab a gas can and leave it somewhere dangerous – near the doorway to a building you think will be occupied, for example, or near a Loot Chest. Find some nearby cover, and hide and wait. When another player gets close enough, train your sights on the gas can and fire to give them something of a hot, fiery surprise.

SLASH AND BURN

Using flames can also be a good tactic if you spot someone in the storm trying to reach safety. Using Firefly Jars or a Flare Gun to set fire to trees and foliage round the edge of the storm circle can give those further behind you a difficult choice between running through the fire, or taking a longer route to safety. Both options can lead to an elimination!

TOP STAR WARS SKINS!

ONCE UPON A TIME, IN A GALAXY FAR, FAR AWAY... THESE AWESOME SKINS BECAME AVAILABLE IN FORTNITE! HERE ARE SOME OF OUR FAVOURITE STAR WARS-THEMED SKINS. KEEP AN EYE OUT FOR THEM IN THE ITEM SHOP!

STAR WARS SERIES | OUTFIT
REY
A scavenger, now studying the Jedi ways.
Part of the **The New Trilogy** set.
Introduced in **Chapter 2, Season 1**.

1,500
GET V-BUCKS
BUY AS A GIFT

REY
TYPE: Star Wars Series **COST:** 1,500 V-Bucks
The new hope for the Jedi, Rey is available in her white robes as a Fortnite skin.

STAR WARS SERIES | OUTFIT
FINN
Former stormtrooper and now committed Resistance member.
Part of the **The New Trilogy** set.
Introduced in **Chapter 2, Season 1**.

1,500
GET V-BUCKS
BUY AS A GIFT

FINN
TYPE: Star Wars Series **COST:** 1,500 V-Bucks
Everyone's favourite ex-Stormtrooper, Finn is ready to lead the Resistance on the Island!

STAR WARS SERIES | OUTFIT
BOBA FETT
A simple man making his way through the galaxy like his father before him.
Part of the **Book of Boba Fett** set.
Introduced in **Chapter 3, Season 1**.
[Built-in], *[Reactive]*

1,500
GET V-BUCKS
BUY AS A GIFT

BOBA FETT
TYPE: Star Wars Series
COST: 1,500 V-Bucks
The famed bounty hunter arrived on the Island in Chapter 3 Season 1, and looks perfectly at home among the foliage.

ZORII BLISS

TYPE: Star Wars Series **COST:** 1,500 V-Bucks
Once a neutral spice runner, Zorii Bliss reconnected with Poe Dameron and played a crucial role in the destruction of the First Order.

If you go after her, you won't make it past sunrise.
Part of the **Book of Boba Fett** set.
Introduced in **Chapter 3, Season 1.**

1,500
GET V-BUCKS
BUY AS A GIFT

FENNEC SHAND

TYPE: Star Wars Series **COST:** 1,500 V-Bucks
A female mercenary and bounty hunter, Fennec is as at home with a Sniper Rifle as she is with a Shotgun!

KRRSANTAN

TYPE: Star Wars Series **COST:** 1,500 V-Bucks
This black-furred Wookie bounty hunter is the last thing you want to see leaping out of the shadows as you enter the endgame.

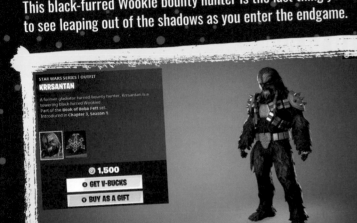

SITH TROOPER

TYPE: Star Wars Series **COST:** 1,500 V-Bucks
With their vivid red armour, there's no mistaking the Sith Trooper – though the skin does tend to stand out against a snowy background.

IMPERIAL STORMTROOPER

TYPE: Star Wars Series **COST:** 1,500 V-Bucks
The ideal skin to select if you prefer to do your fighting in the snowy sections of the map. The classic Imperial Stormtrooper will hopefully be able to hit the target in Fortnite.

KYLO REN

TYPE: Star Wars Series **COST:** 1,500 V-Bucks
One of Hollywood's best bad guys turned good, Kylo Ren cuts a menacing figure if you encounter this skin during a battle!

HIDE AND SEEK

IT MAY NOT BE THE MOST NOBLE WAY TO APPROACH THE GAME, BUT SOMETIMES IT PAYS TO STAY OUT OF SIGHT! THAT WAY, YOU CAN WAIT FOR THE OTHER PLAYERS TO ELIMINATE EACH OTHER BEFORE ONLY NEEDING TO PICK OFF ONE OR TWO SURVIVORS TO CLAIM THE VICTORY ROYALE!

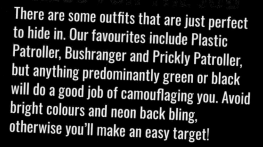

DRESS FOR THE JOB

There are some outfits that are just perfect to hide in. Our favourites include Plastic Patroller, Bushranger and Prickly Patroller, but anything predominantly green or black will do a good job of camouflaging you. Avoid bright colours and neon back bling, otherwise you'll make an easy target!

BUSH CAMPING

It's an oldie, but a goodie. The easiest place to hide is nearly always a large bush. Avoid the very small bushes as your head will still be visible, but head into the middle of a large bush and you'll be almost impossible to spot through the foliage. However, by looking down your sights, you'll be able to look out and spot anyone coming into range! You can also use the same technique in long grass but be careful – moving in long grass causes it to move and it's easier to be spotted!

22

UP A TREE

It's truly amazing how many players don't look up in Fortnite, unless they see a ramp leading them there. Getting yourself on top of a tree can be a great way to avoid detection – you can sometimes drop onto them from a higher structure, or you can use a launchpad or other method of projecting yourself into the air to glide onto the roof. If neither option is available, build a wooden ramp up then shoot out the bottom panel so it disappears. Then simply sit and wait for your opponents to get within range!

IN A VEHICLE

When you are behind the wheel of a vehicle, the engine runs which is a complete giveaway. To avoid that problematic sound, transfer into the passenger seat. The car will be silent, and often players won't take a second glance as they head past – which can give you the chance to eliminate them either by shooting out the window or leaping out to surprise them.

IN A HIDING PLACE

Yeah it's a pretty obvious title! Hiding places in Fortnite are designated features of the landscape. They include Port-a-Potties and Dumpsters and you can opt to hide in one if you are close enough. Be warned, however! They are not foolproof and while you are inside them you will make noises every now and then, which can alert nearby players to your location! They are best used as a short term solution – when fleeing under heavy fire, for example – rather than as part of a strategy.

UNDER STAIRCASES

It's not just monsters in children's storybooks that hide under the stairs! These are often dark locations and players rarely check them. Often you can see through the stairs as well, making it an ideal location to take out an unsuspecting opponent!

23

GUIDE TO BIG VEHICLES

HOW TO MAKE THE MOST OF THE LARGER VEHICLES IN FORTNITE.

WHAT IS A BIG VEHICLE?

As well as the smaller vehicles you'll find around the Island (including cars and lorries), Epic often drops in some bigger, more powerful vehicles. Making the most of these, which are usually only available for a limited time or just for a specific season, can make a big difference, but there are some rules that apply to almost all the 'bigger' vehicles in the game. Mastering them can be essential!

TRY TO HAVE A TRAVELLING COMPANION

More often than not, the larger vehicles really need at least two players to function effectively. Usually, it's not possible to steer or drive them AND fire at the same time. This can leave you very vulnerable to attack, as you'll need to exit the vehicle to return fire – or change seats, leaving you a sitting duck in the process. That means the larger vehicles don't usually offer the same kind of advantage in solo mode as they do in duos, trios or squads and are usually best left alone.

USE THEM AS COVER

When playing solo, you can jump out of the vehicle and use it as cover when in a firefight. Again, that extra damage they can absorb can come in handy, especially when coupled with the fact they are usually much bigger than a normal car. However, you need to be careful that you don't let them take so much damage that they explode as that will cause you an awful lot of damage if you are too close. Instead, try to use them as cover for a few seconds while you get a fix on your opponents' location before launching a counter-offensive.

MAKE THE MOST OF THE EXTRA ARMOUR

The bigger vehicles such as Choppas and Tanks have a lot of armour, so they CAN be useful if you need to travel a distance through a heavily populated area. They're slower moving than cars but if you have no alternative but to head through a war zone, then the extra damage they can absorb can be helpful.

MOVING BARRIERS

If you are playing with at least one partner, you can also use larger ground-based vehicles as rolling barriers. One or more players can jump out and move alongside the vehicle as it is driven forwards, offering them useful cover across an exposed area. Often it's easier to return fire from the ground than it is to do so from a gun turret because you can be more accurate and change who and what you are aiming at quicker.

THE ROADBLOCK

You can use a large vehicle to block a road, as long as there are barriers either side too – buildings, for example. This can be a useful tactic if you are looking to sit tight and defend a position, and want to stop anyone speeding in using a car. Simply park the vehicle in the game to form a temporary barricade but remember – don't stay too close to it or you'll sustain damage if it gets blown up.

GAMEPLAY TACTICS

THERE'S A LOT TO THINK ABOUT IN FORTNITE – THAT'S WHAT MAKES IT SUCH A GREAT GAME! HOWEVER, THERE ARE SOME TACTICS THAT YOU CAN ALWAYS EMPLOY TO GIVE YOURSELF THE EDGE SO START MAKING NOTES, AND PLOT YOUR WAY TO THAT VICTORY ROYALE!

SURROUND SOUND

The sound in Fortnite is a huge element of the gameplay so if you can, use headphones to play. Not only does this give the rest of the family a break from the sound of gunfire and explosions, it will also help you judge where sounds are coming from. A good set of headphones is a must if you take your Fortnite gaming seriously.

STAY QUIET

Try to crouch and walk whenever you can. Running makes noise and you are far more likely to be spotted that way. Similarly, reloading weapons or changing them constantly makes a sound too, and that might be enough to give you away. Try to make as little noise as possible to avoid being caught!

VISUALISE SOUND

You can give yourself some extra help when it comes to hearing where your opponents are by making sure you can visualise where they are. To do this, go into Settings>Audio>Sound>Visualise Sound Effects. When it is turned on, you'll 'see' players making noises if they are close enough to you, and it can make it easier to figure out exactly where they are. You might also find you get the visual clue when you might have missed the audio on your own, so it's a valuable help.

KEEP MOVING

The thing with Fortnite is that you never know who has you in their crosshairs. You need to play the game as if someone is constantly trying to target you – otherwise you'll be in for a rude shock when someone actually is targeting you.

To that aim, don't move in straight lines. Ever. Zig and zag when running, and throw in a few jumps as well. It will make it much harder for an opponent to target you successfully that way.

RUN, JUMP AND GRAB

Make use of the recent additions to the movement dynamics as much as you can. Sprinting is not just a good way to cross open spaces – if used correctly when under fire from close quarters it can get you to safety and the chance to reassess. Grabbing ledges and pulling yourself up can be a great way to reach just-out-of-reach platforms without building a ramp – the sight and sound of which might bring unwanted attention.

USE HIGH GROUND

Being higher than your opponent is the single biggest advantage you can have in Fortnite. IF you can build to achieve that then do so, but always bear in mind that you should look to take the higher route whenever possible. When you are aiming down on an opponent, they'll find it harder to take cover from your fire. If you have the higher ground, you'll also be able to disappear from their sight by taking a couple of steps back and then reappearing a few yards left or right to take them by surprise!

LIVE OFF THE LAND

There are plenty of items that you can gather from crates on the Island, but don't ever forget that the Island itself is your friend too. In particular, hunting wildlife when you are low on health or shield can get you out of a hole quickly – but look out for mushrooms, fruit, and vegetables too. They are often found in food crates but you can also find them scattered on the floor in certain areas too – make the most of them!

RELOAD BETWEEN FIGHTS

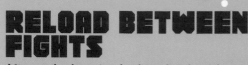

After you've been involved in a battle with another player, it's essential that you reload all your weapons at the earliest possibility. It's easy to forget, especially if you changed weapons during the shootout, but such mistakes can prove fatal in your next combat – when you go to open fire but have an empty chamber. Get into the habit of checking all your weapons and making sure they are all fully loaded so that when you do bump into an opponent, you are ready for them.

REACT WHEN ATTACKED

As you're heading across the map minding your own business, it can really take you by surprise when you take a few hits from an opponent shooting at you. Learn to master your reflexes – rather than panicking, you need to build IMMEDIATELY and throw up a couple of walls to buy yourself vital seconds. If you're playing no build, you need to sprint and slide your way to cover as quickly as you can.

HEAL WITH CARE

Because you need to stay in one spot, you are at your most vulnerable in Fortnite when you are healing. However, there are a few things you can do to make it harder for a sneaky sniper to pick you off. To start with, while you can't move forwards or backwards, you CAN move up and down. As you apply a MedKit or drink a Shield Potion, the simplest thing to do is to keep crouching and standing to make it harder for anyone watching to hit you. However, it's far smarter to make sure that you take cover first (bushes are ideal for this) or build a makeshift hut (with a roof on) so you can heal up without anyone being able to get a cheap shot in.

LEAVE NOTHING BEHIND

If you're not going to use something, try to make sure no-one else can either. Use Chug Splashes or Slurp Barrels as you go past them, even if your health and shield are already maxed out. It may not help you, but the next player to pass through that area might be low on health, and those resources might make all the difference to them. In the same vein, light fires on your way past – especially if racing to the storm circle. It might mean the next player to reach the fire can't relight it – giving you an advantage as they'll be weaker when they make it to the storm circle.

SWITCH WEAPONS IN COMBAT

Reloading in combat is not usually an option. If you're fighting at mid-to-long range then you might be able to take cover and reload, but if you are close to your opponent, then the delay can mean defeat. It's far quicker to switch to another weapon and use that instead, if you have something suitable. For example, if you are using a shotgun but run out of cartridges, switching to an SMG is a far better option that trying to reload.

HARVEST EFFECTIVELY

If you're going to build (and you need to be comfortable with at least the basics) then you'll need materials. Don't wait until late on in the game to gather them. The smaller the storm circle gets, the greater the odds that you'll come under fire while you harvest – and the greater the chances that the noise will give you away.

Try to harvest at the start of the game, so that you have a decent level of materials early on – you'll be glad you did when the game reaches the later stages!

BE PREPARED

Have the right weapon for the right situation. Ideally, you want the right weapon for the job to be in your hand, so you aren't engaging in combat then frantically changing your gun. That means you'll need to change your gun as you go. Crossing an open area where you may come under fire from distance? You'll want a scoped weapon. Moving through a village or town where you might encounter an opponent round the next corner? An SMG is probably the right choice. Entering a building where you might open a door and come face-to-face with another player? That'll be a job for the shotgun. Make sure you're thinking about the type of challenge you might face at any time.

FOOLS RUSH IN

When you've taken the winning shot and your vanquished opponent drops lots of lovely weapons, take a second or two before you go rushing over to it. The sound of a battle will often draw attention to your location, so skipping over to grab some goodies might be just putting yourself in the firing line for someone looking to finish you off. Heal up first if you can, then approach with caution – using cover or builds if you can to minimise the risk!

PEEK ROUND CORNERS

Use the third-person nature of Fortnite to your advantage where you can, by positioning yourself near a corner and using the camera to peek round it. That way, you'll be able to see what's up ahead but anyone looking towards you won't know you're there!

SEE WHAT'S IN STORE

Sometimes you'll be able to see loot on the floor, but it's too far away to judge what it is. However, there's a sneaky little workaround for that. Zoom in with a weapon and tag the loot. Whatever you've tagged will then appear on your HUD so you know if it's worth the risk of heading over to get it.

MASTER YOUR DROPZONES

Don't just drop in randomly. Have three or four pre-determined points that you will always drop to, and master them. Make sure they are well equipped for loot, and that you've identified a suitable back-up option nearby in case things are a little too hot to handle. By dropping into the same places repeatedly, you'll get to know them really well and that inside information can be crucial to making a good start.

UPGRADE AND IMPROVE

Upgrading weapons can be a great way to give yourself an advantage. Always be on the lookout for a better version of the guns you are carrying, but don't worry if you can't find them in the game. If you have enough gold, use the Upgrade Benches around the map to increase the rating of your favourite weapon. It's an often-overlooked strategy that can really pay off in the later stages of a game.

DON'T FORGET THE STORM

Keeping an eye on the storm circle is essential. There are different techniques to playing the storm – we'll cover some of them here – but however you want to play it, make sure you know how much time you have, and how far you have to travel. There is nothing more annoying than winning a protracted battle with another player only to realise the storm will finish you off because you weren't keeping an eye on it.

SIT OUT THEN SWOOP IN

If you come across two players in combat, don't join in immediately. The odds are they will both turn on you and you run a high risk of being take out. Instead, lay low and watch them battle. As soon as one is eliminated, push the position of the other one before they have had a chance to heal. That way you should be able to pick up a relatively easy elimination and pick up the loot dropped by both players!

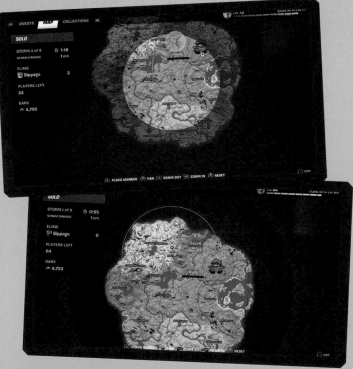

MOVING LATE

An alternative way to play is to deliberately move with the storm just at your back. This approach means you probably won't be attacked from behind, so you can concentrate on what is in front of you. However, be careful – the new storm circle is never central to the old one. If you're in the larger section between the two circles, the storm will move faster for you than it will if you're on the smaller side, so you need to gauge how fast you need to move. If you play this method, it's often worth carrying MedKits in case you misjudge the storm's speed.

MOVING QUICK AND EARLY

One way to deal with the storm is to try and minimise how much you have to move. This means you will be less likely to be spotted by other players as you move across the map, and gives you more chance to find or build cover and pick them off as they move. If you want to play like this then it pays to land fairly central on the Island so you're less likely to have to move long distances. When the storm circle is revealed, get into it (and again, try to head for fairly near the middle of it to minimise further journeys). Use vehicles or launch pads if needed to speed things along, then sit tight and wait as the other players run for the circle.

SOLO TACTICS

THE ORIGINAL BATTLE ROYALE PITS YOU, ALONE, AGAINST 99 RIVALS TO SEE WHO COMES OUT ON TOP. WITH NO-ONE TO HELP YOU, YOU'LL NEED TO BE COMPLETELY SELF SUFFICIENT FROM THE MOMENT YOUR BOOTS HIT THE GROUND. HERE ARE SOME HANDY HINTS THAT MIGHT COME IN USEFUL.

COLLECT QUICKLY

Without squadmates, you need to stand on your own two feet, and quickly. Find landing spots that are well populated with Loot Chests and memorise the most likely places they will appear so that you can quickly gather together a reasonable payload.

GRAB EVERYTHING AT THE START

When you land, grab everything you find until your inventory is full, and only then start making judgement calls about which weapons you need and want. It's vital you don't leave anything behind on those first few seconds as it might just turn out to be the weapon picked up by the player five seconds behind you that they then use to eliminate you!

GATHER AMMO

It's easy to be attracted by the shiny loveliness of the Loot Chests, but it is crucial to remember those guns need ammunition! Look out for ammo boxes and open as many as you can, even if you think you have plenty. Loading up heavy on ammunition early on is safer as you are less likely to be seen by other players. There's no more annoying feeling than getting to the last four or five, having an Epic weapon in your inventory, and not having enough ammunition to use it.

ENTER BUILDINGS HIGH

It may be traditional to enter a building via the front door, but you can forget that in Fortnite! The value of being higher than a opponent is significant, so you will need to think laterally. Build ramps or climb up the outside of buildings so that you can enter from the top and work your way down. Entering at ground level will hand all the advantage to anyone already in the building.

LOOK OUT FOR ACTIVITY

As the game progresses, the landscape around you will change. Get accustomed to looking out for clues about what has happened in an area before you get there. If the door to a building is left open, someone might be in there. Opened chests and damaged buildings suggest the same thing.

You should also be alert to signs of recent occupation – a still-lit campfire, for example, or a structure that you can see is still being assembled. These are signs that an opponent is nearby, so exercise caution. Similarly, if you want to remain undetected, try to avoid leaving such clues by closing doors behind you and only harvesting internal walls for materials so it can't be seen from the outside.

DUOS TACTICS

THE INTRODUCTION OF A PARTNER ADDS A WHOLE NEW ELEMENT TO FORTNITE! HERE'S HOW TO WORK TOGETHER BETTER.

IT'S GOOD TO TALK

Lone wolves don't last five minutes in a game of duos. If you don't work together as a team, you'll be eliminated very quickly. That means it's vital you communicate clearly with your teammate. If you are playing with someone you know, then use voice chat but if not, you can still use ingame emotes to communicate plans. Using the marker on the map to highlight where to land and where to move next is also important, as is tagging any potential risks to you as a pair.

SHARE THE LOAD

In duos, you need to share out the loot you find. With only two of you, it makes sense to more or less mirror each other's payloads because you don't have the numbers to allow any further specialisation. Both players should make sure they have weapons to cater for short- and medium-range combat at the very least, as well as heals. This is one area where it does make sense to carry different things, however, with one player carrying Shield Potions and the other carrying MedKits so you are covered for all eventualities. It's important to share ammo too so neither of you runs out, and be sensible – if your partner has a shotgun and you don't, give them your shotgun shells!

NOT TOO CLOSE

While it is important to stay close to each other in Duos, don't take that too literally. If you are next to each other, or taking cover in the same room or small building, you'll make easy targets. A single explosive will be able to damage you both at the same time, and it will be easy for opponents to focus their fire on you. Stay in sight of each other by all means, but don't get TOO close, so that you can cover each other and make life harder for any other duos looking to target you.

RES WITH CARE

Take care when reviving your partner and try to avoid doing so until the other team are gone – even if that means hiding from them until they go. You'll be defenceless while you res them, and that spells danger. The same applies when using a reboot van – you need to be sure that the coast is completely clear first!

FOCUS YOUR FIRE

When you encounter another duo, it is best to tag one of them and for BOTH of you to fire at that player. This will result in that player being knocked quicker, leaving only one player left for you to focus on. Even if that player has full health and shields, the numerical difference should be enough to swing the battle in your favour. You'll also be able to draw their fire in turn while your partner heals or reloads.

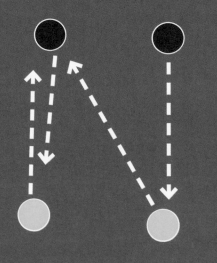

FLANK OPPONENTS

Try to operate so that one of you is designated as the lead contact, with the other assigned to flank your opponents. The lead player will open fire from cover, drawing the attention of the other players. While the battle rages, the second player should sneak round the side of the opponents and open fire. This will often bypass any cover they have taken and the element of surprise can be enough to secure victory!

TRIOS TACTICS

WHOEVER SAID THREE'S A CROWD CLEARLY HASN'T PLAYED FORTNITE TRIOS! THE EXTRA PLAYER MAKES A BIG DIFFERENCE FROM DUOS, SO IT'S A GOOD JOB WE'RE HERE TO SHOW YOU HOW IT'S DONE!

PLAY AGGRESSIVELY

In trios, there are more players in any one area, as it's very unusual for a player to head off on their own in this game mode. In Duos, players separate and in Squads, it's not unusual for teams to split into two pairs. In Trios, however, you'll nearly always find the whole group together – so you need to be aggressive in your play. Trios is probably the most action-packed of the standard game modes, so you'll need to push a little quicker and harder than in most other versions of the game – be ready for it!

PLAY TOGETHER

As already mentioned, there are very few players on their own in Trios – pretty much everyone moves around the map in a three. For that reason, you MUST do the same with your team mates. Heading off alone is not going to end well, so stay in eye contact at all times!

HAVE A PLAYER ON POINT

The best way to move in Trios is in a triangle, with one player out in front acting as the point. Using this method, if the lead player comes under attack, the two supporting players should be able to provide covering fire. Because you aren't all standing close to each other, this will mean your opponents have to fire in different directions to hit you all, and should mean you can avoid being taken out quickly in an ambush.

DUAL RES

In Trios, both players can res a player who has been knocked, and you should make the most of this when it's safe to do so. The numerical disadvantage to being a player down is quite significant, so the sooner you can get your downed comrade back on their feet again, the better your chances of victory become!

HIT AND RUN

One thing to try and avoid is long drawn-out firefights, especially while there are plenty of other teams active. If the team you are engaging with are dug in somewhere and you can't finish them off or push easily, then move on and leave them. Because Trios is quite an aggressive game mode, there's a very good chance that you'll attract the attention of other teams and the last thing you want is to be caught in the middle of a six-person crossfire.

FOCUS YOUR FIRE

Work as a team to focus your aim on one player in an opposing team at a time. If you can knock them quickly, the difference between three players firing on two is significant and it should turn the battle in your favour.

FINISH HIM

If you do manage to knock another player, make sure their team doesn't res them. That doesn't mean you should focus on the knocked player, but you should keep an eye out to make sure no-one is making a move to help them. Again, it's about keeping and maintaining that numerical advantage!

SQUADS TACTICS

WITH FOUR PLAYERS, THE ACTION IS FAST AND FURIOUS – SO YOU'LL NEED OUR GUIDE TO THE SNEAKIEST TIPS AND TACTICS. REMEMBER THAT SOME OF THE TIPS FOR DUOS AND TRIOS WILL ALSO APPLY HERE!

USE VEHICLES

With four of you, you can really make the most of the vehicles in the game. With one of you driving, the others can all fire on any opponents you encounter. It's also possible to stand ON vehicles, rather than inside them, which is a useful tactic to employ when travelling long distances. Not only does it mean you can jump off quickly, you also tend to have a better field of fire. However, don't overuse cars as it puts you all in close proximity to each other and a grenade can put an end to all of you!

SPECIALISE

The extra players available in squads means it's not as sensible to all carry the same things. Ideally, look to specialise a little if you have players who can play specific roles. It makes sense for everyone to carry one close- and one medium-range weapon, but beyond that, make sure the group has variety. One player should use a sniper and stick to cover behind the others, while another could load up with explosives. It makes sense for everyone to have at least one slot for heals, but you can always load one player up as a 'medic' so they have more slots for carrying medical supplies.

SPLIT INTO PAIRS

It often makes sense to work as two pairs, sticking within eyesight of each other. If you stick together as a four, you'll be in big trouble as it is far too easy to be surrounded and picked off. By working as two pairs, you'll have someone close enough to help and res you, but you'll also be able to draw the fire of any other group of players into different directions. It will make you much harder to hit.

DON'T RES

It sounds crazy but don't res your team mates if they are knocked in a fight, unless you have a strong numbers advantage at that point. With potentially three players still in the game, resing is a risk you should avoid – instead, work as a three to even the sides.

SURROUND THEM IN SILENCE

Should you find another squad that have dug in to defend a location, employ some stealth and try and surround them. If you can co-ordinate yourselves so you all open fire at the same time from four different directions, it can completely disorientate the other group and leave them very vulnerable.

PLAN YOUR ATTACKS

If you spot someone on the horizon, don't just ping a shot at them and hope. You need to work out plans of attack so that you all know what you are doing – you can be much more tactical in squads. For example, all training your weapon on an opponent from cover and firing at the same time can knock them before they even know you are there – firing on your own will just alert them to your presence and they will be behind cover before your team mates can join in.

DRESS TO IMPRESS

If you can, wear the same skins and back bling. It can really confuse opponents because they won't be able to tell quickly who they have hit, which makes it harder for them to subsequently focus their fire on the injured player.

TOP SPORTING SKINS!

THE ISLAND MIGHT NOT BE READY TO HOST THE OLYMPICS ANY TIME SOON, BUT IT REMAINS HOME TO A VARIETY OF SPORTING FIGURES. HERE ARE SOME OF OUR FAVOURITES!

FASTBALL

TYPE: Rare **COST:** 1,200 V-Bucks
If she's as accurate with a Sniper Rifle as she is with a baseball then your opponents will be in trouble as you take this skin into battle.

RARE | OUTFIT
FASTBALL
Another victory is on deck.
Part of the **Three Strikes** set.
Introduced in **Season 8**.

1,200
GET V-BUCKS
BUY AS A GIFT

UNCOMMON | OUTFIT
WHISTLE WARRIOR
Throw a flag on the play.
Introduced in **Season 6**.

800
PURCHASE
BUY AS A GIFT

BIRDIE

TYPE: Uncommon **COST:** 800 V-Bucks
Don't let the innocent look fool you — this female golfer is only too happy to swap her six-iron for a shotgun and fire a hole in one of her opponents.

UNCOMMON | OUTFIT
BIRDIE
No mulligans required.
Part of the **Teed Off** set.
Introduced in **Season 8**.

800
PURCHASE
BUY AS A GIFT

WHISTLE WARRIOR

TYPE: Uncommon **COST:** 800 V-Bucks
Ever wanted to take revenge on a referee for a terrible call against your sports team? Well if you see this skin in a game, you'll finally get your wish!

MATCH POINT

TYPE: Uncommon **COST:** 800 V-Bucks
Grab an SMG and get ready to make a racquet with this tennis-themed skin! The white is actually handy camouflage against the snow too!

SPIKE

TYPE: Epic **COST:** 1,500 V-Bucks
Fresh from a game of gridiron, Spike's armour might stop the impact from big tackles, but it's no match for a Light Machine Gun!

ALPINE ACE

TYPE: Epic **COST:** 1,500 V-Bucks
The Island is home to plenty of mountains, so the Alpine Ace skin will feel right at home. It's a brightly coloured one though, so you won't be blending in!

PAR PATROLLER

TYPE: Uncommon **COST:** 800 V-Bucks
Fresh off the fairway, Par Patroller's experience of rooting around in the undergrowth looking for errant shots might serve him well.

SLUGGER

TYPE: Rare **COST:** 1,200 V-Bucks
With his brute power, Slugger is swapping a baseball bat for a Shotgun – expect him to still be involved late into the innings.

SURF RIDER

TYPE: Rare **COST:** 1,200 V-Bucks
Riding the crest of a wave, this skin is a must if you prefer spending time on the water round the Island to hiding on the Island itself.

TEAM RUMBLE TACTICS

IT'S 50 PLAYERS PER TEAM AND RESPAWNS ARE ON. IT'S FAST AND FURIOUS, SO LOCK AND LOAD AND LET'S GET READY FOR BATTLE!

TOOL UP EARLY

Finding weapons in the zone is difficult because there's so much happening. Opening chests or harvesting is a risk because you could easily be shot while you do it – so make sure you are harvesting and looking for loot on your way there, rather than arriving with nothing and hoping to kit yourself out there!

HELP TO HEAL

Being knocked isn't a problem, not being eliminated is. That means playing defensively can help your team just as much as making an elimination. If you see a team mate has been knocked, try to defend them – build around them and heal them up if you can, because you're effectively denying your opponents a point if you do so!

CONTROL SUPPLY DROPS

Supply drops can completely change the momentum of a game of Team Rumble, so dominating the areas they arrive in can be crucial. Working with your team mates to get into position and then building structures round the area to protect it is a smart move, ensuring it's your team that gets its hands on those juicy new weapons that have just arrived.

WORK IN TEAMS IF YOU CAN

With 50 strangers on each side, formulating any kind of clear tactical approach can be absolute mayhem. In fact, it's pretty much impossible. You'll find it much more fruitful if you can jump into a squad with one, two or three of your buddies and join a 50-a-side team that way. At least you'll be able to work cohesively as a smaller group and help each other out.

BIDE YOUR TIME

If you can't find a decent weapon, then play smart and avoid conflict. You'll only end up being eliminated quickly (and probably repeatedly) and that will damage your team's score. Lay low and skirt round the outside of the battles until you have managed to acquire some weapons that make it worth your while to enter the fray.

RANDOM GRENADES

A grenade thrown by you can't hurt your team mates, so if you have some in your inventory that you want to replace with something else, don't just drop them – throw them! Even if you can't target anyone in the battle, you'll be surprised how often a randomly thrown grenade can get lucky in the middle of a hectic battle and take out an opponent – or at least cause them plenty of damage.

STAY IN YOUR LANE

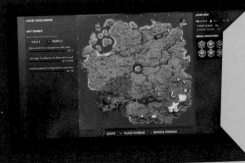

Both teams will start from opposite ends of the Island, with the battle lines drawn in the middle. Try to avoid landing on your opponents' side of the battle early in the fight, because it's too confusing. Instead, stay on the same side as most of your team mates, which will keep your opponents where you want them – in front of you!

COMPLETE CHALLENGES

The sheer volume of players means that Team Rumble is a great opportunity to complete challenges that might take a lot longer in solo mode. It's one of the quickest ways to boost your XP so it's well worth investing some time playing it. For newcomers, it's also a great way to get more bang for your V-Buck – there's no chance of being blasted with a shotgun as soon as you land and finding yourself the first player out of the game. Instead, you can be sure of a fast and furious fighting experience!

FORTNITE IMPOSTERS

A NEW GAME MODE THAT IMITATES THE VIRAL HIT AMONG US IS ANOTHER PERMANENT ADDITION TO THE FORTNITE ROSTER! CHECK OUT OUR TIPS AND TRICKS!

EPIC'S ANSWER TO AMONG US

During the Covid-19 lockdown, a previously unknown game called Among Us, from developers InnerSloth, became a smash hit after YouTubers and Twitch streamers started uploading videos of the game. The premise was simple – players were marooned in space, and some of their number (usually one, but up to three) were actually alien imposters. The imposters have to kill the crewmates, while the crewmates need to figure out who the imposters are and eject them from the ship.

It sounds simple, but the simplicity was what made the game grow very quickly indeed as more and more people got into

playing it. In August 2001, Epic surprised everyone by launching a very similar game called Imposters as a Limited Time Mode in Fortnite. It proved so popular that it has been added to the permanent roster, but not everyone was pleased about it.

Surprisingly for Epic, given their long history of collabs with all kinds of brands, InnerSloth hadn't been invited to work with them on the new game mode. After threats of legal action and tension between the companies, it seems all is well now and there's even Among Us back bling available now!

Here's how to make the most of it!

WHAT'S IT ALL ABOUT?

The premise is the same as Among Us, with eight Agents and two Imposters in each game. The Agents need to identify and expel the two Imposters while completing tasks. When a player is killed, they leave a fragment behind – those who find the fragment can call an emergency meeting, where they can decide who – if anyone to evict from the map.

VOICE CHAT

You can play two version of Imposters – with voice chat and without. Voice chat makes it easier, as you can talk to players in the game if you are standing near enough to them. That can make it easier for you to communicate if you suspect a certain player, but it's safest to play the game without voice chat if you are under 18.

BATTLE BUS REPAIR

SPOTTING AN IMPOSTER

If you are playing as a Crewmate, you'll need to know the tell-tale signs that identify an Imposter. To start with, look out for players who try to get away from a group. Imposters tend not to be too keen on hanging around in groups as it makes it harder for them to get away with making a kill.

You should also look out for any players who you see leaving an area where a body is discovered. If they didn't report the body themselves, it suggests they might be responsible for the death.

Watch other players as they complete tasks and learn how long the tasks generally take. If someone is taking too long to complete a task, or they finish it too quickly, they might well be an Imposter.

Follow those you suspect, but don't get too close. You might catch them in the act but if you are too eager and get too close to them, you might find that you are their next kill. Try to stay a distance back, and in sight of other players to discourage any dastardly deeds from happening.

BEING AN IMPOSTER

If you are one of the two players charged with eliminating all the Crewmates, then there are a few things you can do to tip the odds in your favour.

Firstly, pay attention to your surroundings. The quickest way to lose is to be caught in the act, so make sure you know who is in the same room as you and act quickly and decisively when you get the chance to make a kill.

As a rule it's best to leave the area quickly so that you aren't caught red-handed standing over a body, but sometimes it might be necessary to report the kill yourself to avoid suspicion.

In the emergency meetings, try to avoid accusing anyone else of being the Imposter too quickly. Its best to play dumb and let others lead the accusations. If you try to frame someone who is innocent from the start, then it will look very suspicious if they are ejected and found to be innocent. For that reason, even if you are accusing another player, try to avoid outright lies – "I saw X kill Y" for example – because you'll be caught out. Be more subtle about it – claim you think X was in the same room as Y instead, but don't go too far with your accusations.

Lastly, it's important to look and act helpful. Pretend to complete tasks and don't get caught standing around doing nothing – it makes you look like you are just waiting around for your next kill, so keep moving while you plot your next move!

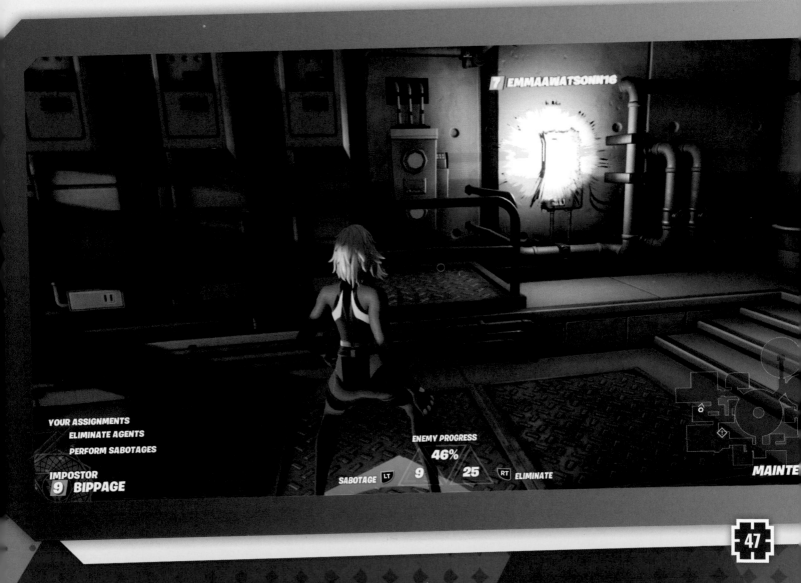

YOUR ASSIGNMENTS
ELIMINATE AGENTS
PERFORM SABOTAGES

IMPOSTOR
9 BIPPAGE

ENEMY PROGRESS
46%

SABOTAGE LT 9 25 RT ELIMINATE

MAINTE

TOP CLASSIC SKINS!

FORTNITE ISN'T JUST ABOUT COLLABS AND GETTING INSPIRATION FROM ELSEWHERE! HERE'S A LOOK AT SOME OF OUR FAVOURITE SKINS.

COBB

TYPE: Rare **COST:** 1,200 V-Bucks

There's nothing sweet about this corn. Cobb is a classic Fortnite favourite. Feels a bit odd eating corn for health when using this skin, however.

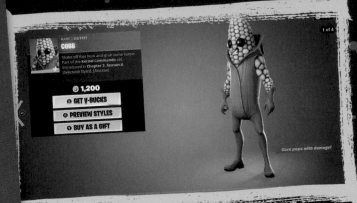

HAYSEED

TYPE: Uncommon **COST:** 800 V-Bucks

He may look like a harmless hillbilly, but this NPC-turned skin is dangerous far beyond mere bad banjo playing.

DUMMY

TYPE: Rare **COST:** 1,200 V-Bucks

This cool skin has more to offer than simply crashing cars. Landing in Chapter 2 Season 3, he quickly became a very popular choice and is still used widely to this day.

B.R.U.T.E. GUNNER

TYPE: Uncommon **COST:** 800 V-Bucks

With her sleek outfit and futuristic helmet, B.R.U.T.E. Gunner became an immediate fan favourite when she landed way back in Season X.

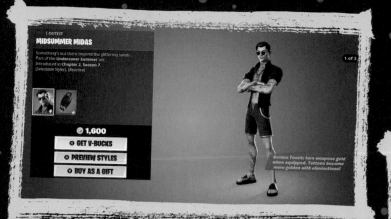

THE BRAT

TYPE: Rare **COST:** 1,200 V-Bucks
Choose this skin and you'll feel anything but a silly sausage! The Brat is one of the most-loved Fortnite skins so expect to run into him a fair few times!

MIDSUMMER MIDAS

TYPE: Epic **COST:** 1,600 V-Bucks
One of the main characters in the Chapter 2 storyline that resulted in huge changes to the Island, even Midas wants to kick back and relax by the pool sometimes.

DJ BOPP

TYPE: Legendary **COST:** 2,000 V-Bucks
Ain't no party like a llama party! This awesome skin brings the party wherever she goes, and dates all the way back to Chapter 7!

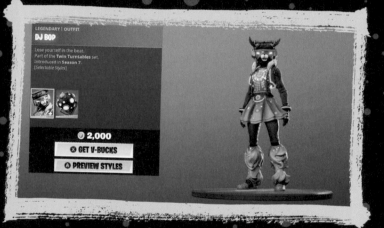

BEACH BRUTUS

TYPE: Rare **COST:** 1,300 V-Bucks
Midas' henchman is no different to his boss – he loves a beach break too. Pack that hulking frame into his swimming trunks and away you go!

PLASTIC PATROLLER

TYPE: Uncommon
COST: 1800 V-Bucks
Perhaps the closest skin Fortnite has to pay-to-win, Plastic Patroller is perfect for blending into the background. Opponents will often walk straight past you without noticing you!

DIFFERENT WAYS TO PLAY FORTNITE!

IT'S NOT JUST ABOUT BATTLE ROYALE! IF YOU WANT SOMETHING A LITTLE DIFFERENT FROM YOUR FORTNITE EXPERIENCE, THEN HERE ARE SOME OTHER WAYS YOU CAN GET YOUR FIX!

COMPETITIVE

If you want to get competitive, then you need move into Arena mode. It's available in Solo, Duos and Trios mode, and plays the same way that Battle Royale does. However, if you perform well you'll be rewarded with Hype points. The more Hype you win, the higher league you are placed in, and the better the players you are paired with will be. Eventually, if you're good enough, you can even play for cash prizes but be warned – the standard is very high and you will absolutely need to have mastered the art of building if you want to reach those heady heights!

There are also competition days for solos and duos on a weekly basis. Usually these last for two rounds over two days. On day one, the tournament is open to all, and on day two, the top hundred players can log back in to duke it out for top spot.

On top of this, there are also one-off competitions and more – keep an eye on the 'Competitive' tab in the game so you know what's happening when!

BUILD FIGHTS

Playing a Build Fights mode is an excellent way to improve your building skills. Typically these games will place you in a very small area, with your mats already maxed out. You'll need to build up, around and over an opponent – who'll be trying to do exactly the same to you!

By helping you master the art of building, this game mode is more than just a game in its own right – it can help make you a better player in Fortnite too! Many build modes are one-on-one gameplay only, but some feature more players for you to take on!

DEATHRUNS

It's not the cheeriest of names, is it? Finding yourself embarking on a Deathrun game sounds more than a little intimidating – and so it should be! Deathrun maps are basically designed for players to run through, avoiding obstacles and traps that are designed exclusively to kill them.

This will often involve speed, but the best deathruns will also challenge your brain as you figure out ways round obstacles, and there's a lot of balancing and well-timed jumps as well. Most deathruns are pretty forgiving, with regular checkpoints should you end up falling into a trap – with infinite lives to help you keep going until you finally figure it out.

Playing Deathruns can help increase your speed and ability to escape enemy fire in Battle Royale, so they are a useful training tool as well as great fun!

VEHICLES

If your favourite part of a Battle Royale is tearing round the Island in a vehicle, then you might like to know there are plenty of games that are based exclusively around using vehicles. Some are based on the driver vs sniper idea, where players in vehicles have to avoid players shooting at them, while others are just good old fashioned races round a track in a race to the finish line!

You can also play demolition derbies, where the aim is to smash up and eliminate all the other cars to leave you as the last player standing!

Whichever game mode you play, you'll find it's a great way to get to grips with a variety of vehicle types, meaning you'll be in a better position when it comes to using them in the main game. There are even Choppa races, as well as game modes that focus on tanks and other large vehicles.

PARKOUR

One of the more exciting recent additions to Fortnite has been the extra movement options, giving you the chance to sprint, slide and climb in the game. The only thing that keeps up with how quickly Epic can make changes to Fortnite is how quickly the creative community can come up with new ideas for playing the game – so it's little surprise to see that there are already plenty of Parkour games to play. Some are similar to Deathruns, while others just give you an open-world map to try and rack up a highscore in – think Tony Hawk without the skateboard.

SURVIVAL

ZOMBIE ISLAND
NATURAL DISASTER SURVIVAL

Of course, Fortnite's origins were as a survival game – Escape the World – and so it's no surprise that there are plenty of games based on surviving as long as you can. Many of these will involve outlasting successive waves of enemies that increase in numbers, frequency and toughness and, as is traditional, they very often feature zombies as the enemy!

PARTY GAMES

Fortnite doesn't always have to be about competition and eliminating everyone else. Sometimes, you just want to chill with your friends and catch up without worrying about someone surprising you with a shotgun. If that's your thing, there are plenty of ways to socialise in Fortnite.

One is the classic and simple Party Royale mode, which is probably the best known. But there are plenty of alternatives, each with their creator's take on the world – you and your Fortnite buddies are bound to find somewhere that is the perfect home for you! You can play football, watch films, race cars or just kick back and catch up – the decisions are all yours!

TOP ANIMAL SKINS!

THE ISLAND IS TEEMING WITH WILDLIFE – SO WHY NOT ADD SOME MORE INTO THE MIX BY SELECTING AN ANIMAL SKIN! HERE ARE SOME OF OUR FAVOURITES!

GROWLER

TYPE: Epic **COST:** 1,500 V-Bucks
This doggy is anything but a good boy, with teeth that would strike fear into anyone's heart!

HEARTBREAKER

TYPE: Rare **COST:** 1,200 V-Bucks
Fortnite is the home of the llama, so you may as well join the party. This particular mammal cuts a suave figure, and is guaranteed to break more than just hearts!

JELLIE

TYPE: Rare **COST:** 1,200 V-Bucks
One thing you can't accuse THIS jellyfish of is lacking a backbone! Jellie's translucent body makes him easy to see coming though, but he's right at home in the water!

FENNIX

TYPE: Rare **COST:** 1,200 V-Bucks
To win at Fortnite, you need to show some cunning – so who better to play as than a fox?! Fennix's wily ways might just give you the edge.

MOISTY MERMAN

TYPE: Legendary **COST:** 2,000 V-Bucks
This merman suit sticks out like a sore thumb on land – but it's very hard to see you coming if you stick to the watery parts of the Island!

BIGFOOT

TYPE: Rare **COST:** 1,200 V-Bucks
He may be one of the most-hunted phenomena in the world, but no-one has captured Bigfoot yet. Do you think you could be the one to bring him in?

KING FLAMINGO

TYPE: Uncommon
COST: 800 V-Bucks
Remember what we told you about blending in and going unnoticed as much as possible? Forget that if you choose this skin – a bright pink, feathery exhibition!

DARK REX

TYPE: Dark Series **COST:** 1,200 V-Bucks
It's not just modern day beasts on the Island, you know. This dino-inspired skin helps you take it (very) old school!

TENDER DEFENDER

TYPE: Epic **COST:** 1,500 V-Bucks
This finger-lickin' assassin is a great choice for the player who likes to stand out. Unless of course, you're... chicken?

QUICK BUILD GUIDE

THE WALL

THEY DON'T GET MUCH EASIER THAN THIS. IF YOU COME UNDER FIRE, THESE ARE THE STEPS YOU NEED TO TAKE – QUICKLY!

STEP ONE

Spin round to face the direction that the gunfire came from and build two walls next to each other quickly.

STEP TWO

If you decide staying to fight is not the best move but you are in open ground, then head towards cover BACKWARDS building more simple walls as you go to keep cover between you and the shooter.

THE RAISED RAMP

ANOTHER VERY SIMPLE TECHNIQUE, A RAMP CAN GIVE YOU TWO THINGS – COVER, AND HIGHER GROUND. IF YOU FIND YOURSELF RUNNING HEADLONG TOWARDS AN OPPONENT, THIS IS A WINNER.

STEP ONE

Build a single wall panel a few yards ahead of yourself.

STEP TWO

Build a ramp leading up to the single wall unit you just built.

STEP THREE

You can now run up the ramp to take a higher position. The wall panel you put up will absorb shots first, protecting your ramp from immediate destruction and buying you a few vital extra seconds!

TURTLING

THIS TECHNIQUE CAN BE USED TO COVER YOURSELF WHILE YOU HEAL, OR TO HIDE AWAY WHILE UNDER FIRE (IF YOU HAVE PLENTY OF MATERIALS). IF YOU'RE JUST HEALING, USE WOOD – IF YOU'RE UNDER FIRE YOU'LL NEED BRICK IF POSSIBLE.

STEP TWO

Look up (that's important, otherwise you'll build the roof underneath you) and pop a pyramid roof on the top. You're now covered from all angles!

STEP ONE

Spin round while building walls to build a simple square with you in the middle.

THE TOWER

YOU MAY HEAR THIS REFERRED TO AS 'BUSTING 90s' - A REFERENCE TO THE TURNS YOU NEED TO MAKE IN ORDER TO BUILD HIGH. THIS TAKES MORE PRACTICE THAN THE OTHER SIMPLE BUILDS, BUT IS AN ESSENTIAL ONE TO MASTER.

STEP TWO

Build a ramp heading up, and climb it – staying to the side of the ramp you've chosen.

STEP ONE

Build a square around you, then stand against the back wall on either the far left or far right (try both, one will instinctively feel more comfortable to you).

STEP THREE

Build four more walls, so you are again level below the top.

STEP FOUR

At a 90 degree angle from your first ramp, face into the square (remember, you should be on the right or left of the ramp) and build another ramp up to the top.

STEP FIVE

Climb it, sticking to the same side of the ramp. At the top, repeat the process as often as you like!

ADVANCED BUILDING GUIDE

SO YOU'VE MASTERED THE BASICS! NOW IT'S TIME TO LEARN HOW TO GET A LITTLE MORE ADVANCED WITH YOUR BUILDS!

PRACTICE MAKES PERFECT

The key thing, obviously, is to practice. Building quickly is challenging, but the best way to learn is through practice. That means avoiding Battle Royale for a while and practicing – either in specific building game modes created by Epic or other players, or heading into Battle Lab and practicing on an empty Island.

HARVEST LIKE MAD

If building is a key part of your game, you need to build gathering materials into your gameplay as secondary nature. You'll burn through supplies quickly, so take time after each battle to replenish your supplies. Remember too that you can recycle some supplies by destroying your own builds if you have won the battle and are now moving on!

LEARN TO EDIT

This is a gamechanger. Practice editing windows and doors into your builds, so that you can build, edit a gap for yourself, shoot through it, then close the window again. Try to make this such a standard activity that it ends up being part of your muscle memory, meaning you'll be able to do it pretty much instinctively without having to think too much!

58

THE SNIPER TOWER

While a simple tower will offer you good opportunities to take potshots at others, it does leave you a little open to return fire. A sniper tower is a far more advanced idea!

STEP 1

Find high ground. There's no point in a sniper tower at the foot of a mountain, after all.

STEP 2

Build a solid base, from metal or brick. This will make it harder for opponents to destroy the bottom of your build. Keep it metal or brick for at least the first three storeys.

STEP 3

Don't go TOO high, as you'll sustain fall damage if the tower is destroyed. Over six storeys is usually instant death so aim for five at most.

STEP 4

At the top, build your sniper's nest. Sticking with metal or stone, build a ramp outwards from each wall.

STEP 5

Head to the corners of each of your ramps and build a straight wall either side so you can't be shot from the sides, and your sniper's nest is complete!

59

BATTLE PASS PROGRESSION

IF YOU WANT TO UNLOCK ALL THE GOODIES YOU CAN, THEN THIS IS A MUST-READ! MAKE THE MOST OF THE XP AVAILABLE TO LEVEL UP AS QUICKLY AS YOU CAN!

KNOW YOUR CHALLENGES

It's really important that you read and understand the challenges and focus on the quickest ones for the maximum XP. Often there are time-sensitive challenges which may be around for as little as a day, so be sure you know what they are and play games where your focus is on those challenges. If you have to visit a named location, then land there, for example. Know when you are getting close to the end of accumulative challenges (a certain number of headshots, for example, or a distance travelled in a vehicle) and when you are close, then focus on those challenges more than any others.

MAKE THE MOST OF SUPERCHARGED XP

If you don't play for a day or so, you'll be granted Supercharged XP for a short time. Make the most of it! Really focus on completing valuable XP challenges and prioritise big scores. Getting 40,000XP in one go instead of the usual 20,000, for example, makes a big difference. If you play smart, you can line up some challenges so you are close to completing them, then not play for a day. When you log back on, you'll be on an XP boost and will be able to tick off those challenges quickly for extra points.

GRAB THE GOLD

Lots of XP challenges will be made easier if you are grabbing gold whenever you can. Smash sofas to find hidden goodies and loot your vanquished opponents at every opportunity. By having plenty of gold, you'll be able to buy items and interact with NPCs which can often make challenges easier. Some challenges revolve around spending a certain amount or buying a number of items, but others will need you to deal damage with a specific weapon or similar – so having the gold to buy it can make life a lot easier.

TAKE EVERY BOUNTY YOU CAN

Another way to gain gold – and XP – is to ALWAYS take on bounties when you pass a bounty board. If you fail, then you don't lose anything. If you happen to encounter your bounty and eliminate them, you're rewarded with gold AND valuable XP. In fact, even if another player eliminates your bounty, you STILL get gold and XP, which makes it an absolute no-brainer to take out a bounty at every board.

PARTY ASSIST!

You don't have to do everything yourself. If you're playing in a duo, trio or squad, then you'll share in the achievements of your squadmates! If they do something that's part of a challenge you have open, then you'll piggyback their success and find that you gain the XP you would have done if you were playing alone. This means that if you are chasing XP, playing squads can often be the most lucrative way of securing big XP scores!

FORTNITE SETTINGS EXPLAINED

WHICHEVER FORMAT YOU PLAY FORTNITE ON, GETTING THE SETTINGS RIGHT FOR YOU CAN BE A BIT OVERWHELMING. THE DEFAULTS DON'T WORK FOR EVERYONE, SO HERE'S OUR GUIDE TO MAKING CHANGES THAT CAN HELP GIVE YOU THE EDGE.

CONTROLLER OPTIONS

INPUT

CONTROLLER AUTO-RUN	ON
BUILD IMMEDIATELY (BUILDER PRO)	ON
EDIT HOLD TIME	0.100 Seconds
SLIDE HOLD TIME	0.100 Seconds
RESET CAMERA AXES	PITCH
RESET CAMERA TIME	0.100 Seconds
VIBRATION	ON

SENSITIVITY

LOOK SENSITIVITY	4 (NORMAL)
AIM SENSITIVITY (ADS)	4 (NORMAL)
BUILD MODE SENSITIVITY MULTIPLIER	1.7x
EDIT MODE SENSITIVITY MULTIPLIER	1.0x
USE ADVANCED OPTIONS	ON

ADVANCED - LOOK SENSITIVITY

CONTROLLER AUTO-RUN

Turn controller auto-run on/off. When on, double clicking the left stick will make you automatically run forward without needing to hold the stick forward.

OFF
► ON

APPLY   RESET   BACK

MOVEMENT

Turn auto-run OFF, so that you have to make a conscious decision to run. It might sound more complicated, but sometimes you need the ability to stop dead at a moment's notice – when you hear footsteps, for example. With auto-run turned on, it's easy to accidentally run forwards when you don't want to, which can also cause major problems if you are trying to sneak up on an opponent, for example. However, leave toggle sprint to ON – again, this doesn't take control out of your hands but makes it easier for you to switch between the two options.

didn't stick the landing (28 m)

2:31   35   2   2

3920   566   206   43

50
100

30 / 378
STINGER SMG

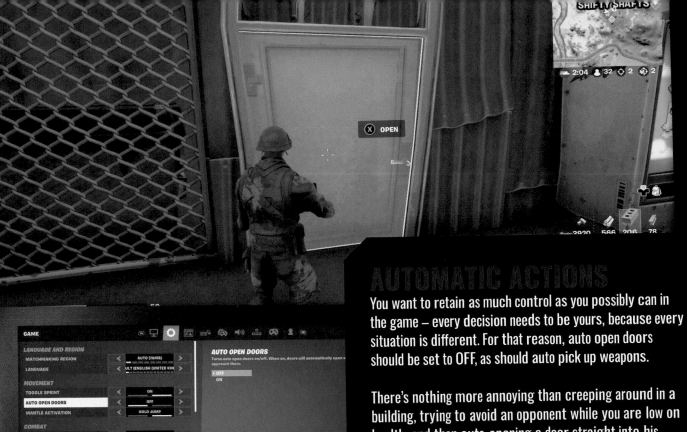

AUTOMATIC ACTIONS

You want to retain as much control as you possibly can in the game – every decision needs to be yours, because every situation is different. For that reason, auto open doors should be set to OFF, as should auto pick up weapons.

There's nothing more annoying than creeping around in a building, trying to avoid an opponent while you are low on health, and then auto-opening a door straight into his shotgun barrel. Similarly, hoovering up loot might seem like an appealing option to automate, but it can mean you pick up the rubbish you don't want first, then have to sort through and drop it quickly. That delay could prove fatal, so turn it off!

MANAGING YOUR INVENTORY

It's absolutely essential that you configure your preferred item slots, so that you get used to where things are. Exactly how you order things will be down to individual taste, but knowing what to press to cycle to your shotgun will soon become muscle memory and if an opponent jumps out of a bush when you least expect it, that could be absolutely crucial to your survival.

Auto-sorting consumables to the right is another individual choice – if you like having your heals to the right, you can turn this on – but if you prefer them to the left, then turn this off.

AIMING BETTER

Firstly, turn aim assist on in these settings. It's not cheating, and you won't gain a huge unfair advantage from it! It will however, help you lock on to an opponent for just a split second when you catch them in your crosshairs, and that can make a significant difference.

Secondly, experiment with different aim sensitivities. Most players will find one of the normal settings works best for them, but play a few matches with each one (giving yourself time to get used to them) before deciding what's the best solution for you.

CONTROL FREAK

Don't forget that you can change the buttons if they don't work for you! Epic has set up some different defaults that can help if your game is based on building or combat, for example, but you have full freedom – so use it!

When it comes to deadzones for your sticks (if you're playing on a console or using a pad) then leave them at around 20%. That means if you accidentally nudge a stick, your view won't suddenly follow the movement. Instead, it takes a fraction more to make your avatar move. While that sounds odd, it's actually really important to stop you moving and looking round by mistake!

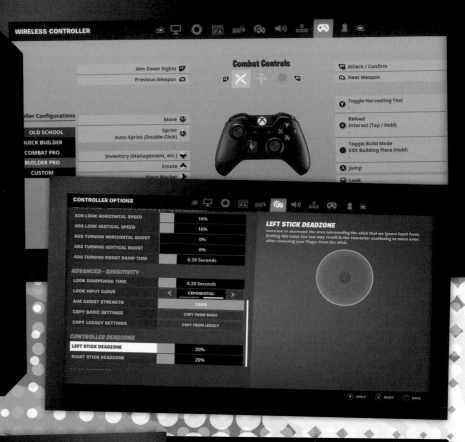

BUILD LIKE A BOSS

Building quickly is key, so it pays to take a little time to set the controls up to help you do so. To build quicker than you ever thought possible, turn Turbo Building to ON. This will continue to build while you look around, and is perfect for quickly building a box or tower should you come under fire. You simply select a wall piece and look round to box yourself in immediately.

EDITING MADE EASY

The ability to quickly edit your buildings can make the difference in a close-run build battle. If you can build a wall, edit a hole in it, blast your opponent, then replace the gap before they can return fire, you're onto a winning strategy.

However, the default controls don't make that especially easy and it can take too long to pull this trick off. To get around that problem, change the hold time for editing to 0.1 seconds, in the controller menus. This will make it much easier for you to quickly edit your builds.

LOOK BEHIND YOU!

The speed you look left and right is another setting that is worth experimenting with. Too fast, and you'll find it harder to target players off to either side of your sights. Too slow, and you can find yourself taking ages to line them up, by which time they will probably have finished you off.

For the best of both worlds, a value of between 15% and 20% is USUALLY best – but play some practice matches yourself and experiment with this until you find the best settings for you.

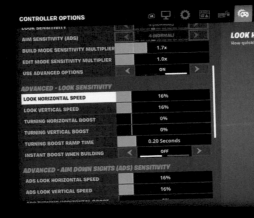

SURROUND SOUND

Two huge advantages you can give yourself when it comes to sound is to turn visualise sound effects to ON so you will see on-screen when there are noises like footsteps or combat nearby. These will often show on screen before you hear them anyway, and help you to be really precise when it comes to knowing where the sound is coming from.

However, you should also use 3D headphones if you can. Sometimes, you'll hear an opponent sneaking, or making a sound that doesn't show up on the visual hints, such as reloading their weapon. Knowing where that sound is coming from can give you the best chance of getting them before they get you!

TOP FORTNITE LEGENDS SKINS!

ONE OF THE GREAT THINGS ABOUT FORTNITE IS HOW IT CAN REPAY THE LOYALTY THAT THE COMMUNITY SHOWS TO IT. ALL THESE IMAGES PAY TRIBUTE TO PEOPLE WHO HAVE CONTRIBUTED TO THAT COMMUNITY IN SOME WAY!

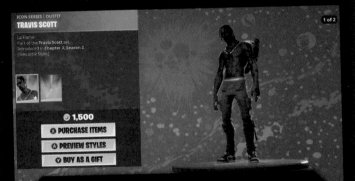

TRAVIS SCOTT

TYPE: Icon Series **COST:** 1,500 V-Bucks
The music legend was given his own skin to celebrate holding a huge concert in the Fortnite universe – a huge step forward for music and gaming!

LOSERFRUIT

TYPE: Icon Series **COST:** 1,500 V-Bucks
The popular YouTuber was given her own skin as part of a celebration of YouTubers in Chapter 2 Season 3!

MAJOR LAZAR

TYPE: Icon Series **COST:** 1,600 V-Bucks
Another musical influencer who has seen the power of Fortnite and used it to reach their fans in a different way.

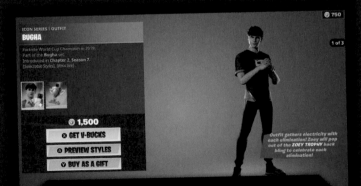

BUGHA

TYPE: Icon Series **COST:** 1,500 V-Bucks
The inaugural Fortnite World Champion was rewarded with his own skin in recognition as being crowned the best player on the planet!

ALI-A

TYPE: Icon Series **COST:** 1,800 V-Bucks
Now you too can join the Ali-A Army and head into battle, with the skin modelled on this popular British YouTube legend.

THEGREFG

TYPE: Icon Series **COST:** 1,500 V-Bucks
Another YouTube legend made the leap to his own skin back in Chapter 2 Season 5!

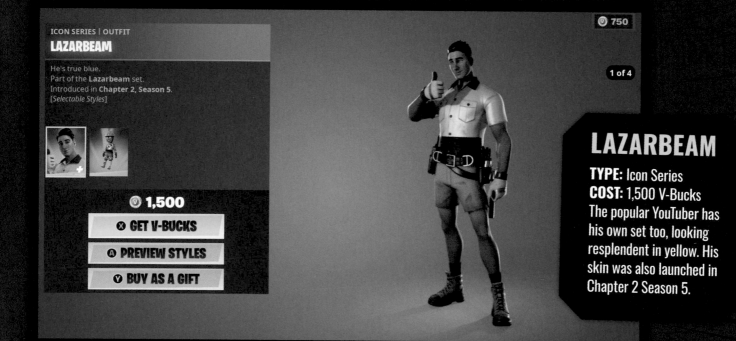

LAZARBEAM

TYPE: Icon Series
COST: 1,500 V-Bucks
The popular YouTuber has his own set too, looking resplendent in yellow. His skin was also launched in Chapter 2 Season 5.

LACHLAN

TYPE: Icon Series **COST:** 1,500 V-Bucks
Lachlan is part of the PWR series, in reference to his gaming brand. This skin landed in Chapter 2 Season 4.

MARSHMELLO

TYPE: Icon Series **COST:** 1,500 V-Bucks
Another musical icon, Marshmello has played in pro-am tournaments as well as holding a concert in Fortnite!

TOP ONLINE FORTNITE STARS!

THE FORTNITE COMMUNITY IS HUGE ONLINE, SO WE'VE SHORTLISTED SOME OF THE BEST STREAMERS TO WATCH AND LEARN FROM!

LAZARBEAM

REAL NAME: Lannan Neville Eacott
TOTAL VIEWS: 7.85 billion

LazarBeam dropped out of school at 15 and started working for his parents' demolition company, where he began his YouTube career by posting slow motion footage of demolitions.

He shot to fame in 2018 as he began posting Fortnite footage and by the end of 2019, he was YouTube's eight-most-viewed content creator of the year, with over 2 billion views. He's noted for his incredible knowledge of Fortnite as well as his funny and irreverent style which sees him sharing memes and comedy sketches.

His YouTube fame even saw him appear as himself in the movie Free Guy – which contains lots of other nods to Fortnite, and like some of his fellow YouTubers, he has also been rewarded with his own Fortnite skin!

LACHLAN

REAL NAME: Lachlan Ross Power
TOTAL VIEWS: 5.2 billion

Lachlan Power started out broadcasting gaming footage of himself playing Minecraft, Battlefield and Call of Duty. However, like many of the YouTubers in this list, he really hit the big time when he started posting about Fortnite. In 2019, he became the first Australian YouTuber ever to hit 10 million subscribers.

He also has his own Fortnite skin, and uses his fame to raise money for charity. He's donated lots of his own money too, including $15,000 to Team Trees, who plant a tree for every dollar they receive, and has also raised money for the Red Cross and a relief fund after the Australian bush fires of 2020.

NINJA

REAL NAME: Richard Tyler Blevins
TOTAL VIEWS: 2.49 billion

Ninja was born in Detroit before moving to Chicago as a child. After he finished high school in 2009, he became a professional eSports player focusing on Halo 3. To start with, he played competitively and did not distract himself with streaming his performances, though his reputation meant he was a well-known online presence.

In 2011 he began streaming – firstly Halo 3, later moving to Player Unknown's Battlegrounds. It was in late 2017 when he switched to playing and streaming Fortnite that his fame grew. Broadcasting on Twitch, he gained 1.5 million new fans in just six months, and has since set several Twitch records.

He's played online with some huge celebrities including Drake, Travis Scott and Marshmello, and has become a celebrity in his own right – Red Bull even put his face on a limited edition can after a sponsored online challenge event! He also appeared in Free Guy as himself, and on the American version of the Masked Singer!

LOSERFRUIT

REAL NAME: Kathleen Belsten
TOTAL VIEWS: 393.7 million

Another Australian YouTube sensation, Loserfruit started out posting videos of League of Legends and Overwatch, before taking up Fortnite in 2017 and seeing her subscriber figures rocket.

She's one of the most followed female YouTubers and Twitch players, behind only Pokimane, and was only the second streamer to be rewarded with her own skin in Fortnite (after Ninja).

She's popular because of her down to earth style and humourous look at the world – something she also shows in her vlogs, which she records under the name Lufu.

ALI-A

REAL NAME: Alastair Aitken
TOTAL VIEWS: 7.65 billion

Ali-A is a British YouTuber from Woking, and is probably as well-known for his Call of Duty videos as he is for his Fortnite work. He also plays a variety of more family-friendly games on his secondary YouTube account which he runs with his partner Clare and features them both playing together.

As well as livestreaming his games, Ali-A also often records walkthroughs and reviews new Call of Duty maps and missions. He's an educated and informed YouTuber who puts time and effort into passing on useful views and information, unlike so many who think that being loud is a substitute for being clever. Check him out!

SuperPoshGrape shotgunned Exhale34
Blaze knocked out Shadow74739 with a shotgun

TOP-UP BONUS 45%

POKIMANE

REAL NAME: Imane Anys
TOTAL VIEWS: 795 million

Pokimane is a Canadian-Moroccan YouTuber who took her name by mixing her own name with her beloved Pokémon. She began streaming on Twitch in 2013, using a PC she bought for $250, after she reached Platinum rank in League of Legends.

She began playing Fortnite in 2018 as part of a sponsorship deal, and her videos were very successful. However, she is streaming Fortnite less often now — though her videos are always well thought out and entertaining.

Like many other internet celebrities, she landed a role in Free Guy as herself — and she's even streamed alongside a US congresswoman who she played Among Us with, in a bid to encourage more people to vote.

DR LUPO

REAL NAME: Benjamin Lupo
TOTAL VIEWS: 129 million

Dr Lupo started out streaming Destiny, before switching to Fortnite. He often streams with others, and he is well-known for his willingness to interact with other streamers and fans. He often streams with Ninja, and has taken part in a number of online charity events, raising $2.3 million for St Jude Children's Research Hospital.

What makes his videos stand out is the detail he goes into about why he makes the decisions he does — rather than just showing how he wins, he explains his tactics and thought process along the way, which can be a useful guide to someone new to the game.

TOP COLLAB SKINS!

EPIC LOVES WORKING WITH OTHER FAMOUS BRANDS, SO THERE ARE SOME AWESOME CHARACTERS FROM GAMES AND MOVIES AVAILABLE. HERE ARE SOME OF OUR FAVES!

MASTER CHIEF

TYPE: Gaming Legends Series
COST: 1,500 V-Bucks
Perhaps the daddy of the modern shooter, Master Chief is here in all his glory from Halo.

GAMING LEGENDS SERIES | OUTFIT
MASTER CHIEF
Master Chief Petty Officer John-117.
Part of the **Master Chief** set.
Introduced in **Chapter 2, Season 5.**

@ 750

@ 1,500
⊗ GET V-BUCKS
⊽ BUY AS A GIFT

Master Chief has arrived on the island. Complete a match on Xbox Cloud Gaming or Xbox Series X|S to unlock a matte black style!

LEGENDARY | OUTFIT
JOHN WICK
Every action has consequences.
Part of the **John Wick** set.
Introduced in **Season 9.**
[Selectable Styles]

2 of 2

@ 2,000
⊗ GET V-BUCKS
⌃ PREVIEW STYLES
⊽ BUY AS A GIFT

2FA required to send gifts

JOHN WICK

TYPE: Legendary
COST: 2,000 V-Bucks
A Fortnite favourite. After an early skin bore a passing resemblance to John Wick, Epic brought out an official one!

RYU

TYPE: Gaming Legends Series
COST: 1,600 V-Bucks
The Street Fighter legend has arrived in Fortnite to show he knows his way round an Assault Rifle as well as being good with his hands.

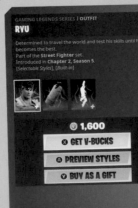

GAMING LEGENDS SERIES | OUTFIT
RYU
Determined to travel the world and test his skills until he becomes the best.
Part of the **Street Fighter** set.
Introduced in **Chapter 2, Season 5.**
[Selectable Styles], [Built-in]

@ 750

1 of 2

@ 1,600
⊗ GET V-BUCKS
⊙ PREVIEW STYLES
⊽ BUY AS A GIFT

Outfit includes the built-in Shoryuken emote!

BLANKA

TYPE: Gaming Legends Series
COST: 1,600 V-Bucks
Street Fighter's green monster is here, and ready to blend in with the foliage on the Island.

GAMING LEGENDS SERIES | OUTFIT
BLANKA
Seeing you in action is a joke!
Part of the **Street Fighter** set.
Introduced in **Chapter 3, Season 2**.
[Built-in], [Selectable Styles]

1,600
- GET V-BUCKS
- PREVIEW STYLES
- BUY AS A GIFT

Blanka-Chan reacts to Eliminations!

GAMING LEGENDS SERIES | OUTFIT
CHUN-LI
Interpol officer with a strong sense of justice and even stronger roundhouse kick.
Part of the **Street Fighter** set.
Introduced in **Chapter 2, Season 5**.
[Selectable Styles], [Built-in]

750

1 of 2

1,600
- GET V-BUCKS
- PREVIEW STYLES
- BUY AS A GIFT

Outfit includes the built-in Lightning Kick emote!

CHUN-LI

TYPE: Gaming Legends Series **COST:** 1,600 V-Bucks
The third legend from Street Fighter to form the set, Chun-Li is as dangerous with weapons as she is with her fists!

KAIT DIAZ

TYPE: Gaming Legends Series **COST:** 1,500 V-Bucks
The Gears Of War legend is new to the Island, but will find it a home-from-home. It shouldn't take her long to master the weaponry available to her.

| OUTFIT
ELLEN RIPLEY
Last survivor of the Nostromo.
Part of the **In Space...** set.
Introduced in **Chapter 2, Season 5**.
[Selectable Styles]

1,500
- GET V-BUCKS
- PREVIEW STYLES
- BUY AS A GIFT

GAMING LEGENDS SERIES | OUTFIT
KAIT DIAZ
Outsider turned soldier in the COG Army and member of Delta-One.
Part of the **Delta-One** set.
Introduced in **Chapter 3, Season 1**.
[Selectable Styles]

1,500
- GET V-BUCKS
- PREVIEW STYLES
- BUY AS A GIFT

ELLEN RIPLEY

TYPE: Epic **COST:** 1,500 V-Bucks
The kick-ass heroine from the Alien films and games, Ellen is not the kind of woman to scare easily, and will do whatever she needs to do in order to survive.

MARCUS FENIX

TYPE: Gaming Legends Series **COST:** 1,500 V-Bucks
One of videogaming's most recognisable icons, Marcus Fenix is the kind of skin that will strike fear into the hearts of any opponent silly enough to stand in his way!

ROBOCOP

TYPE: Epic **COST:** 1,500 V-Bucks
Serve the public trust, protect the innocent and uphold the law. All without leaving Fortnite. What's not to love?

GAMING LEGENDS SERIES | OUTFIT
MARCUS FENIX
Legendary hero of the Pendulum and Locust Wars brought back into the fight by his son.
Part of the **Delta-One** set.
Introduced in **Chapter 3, Season 1**.

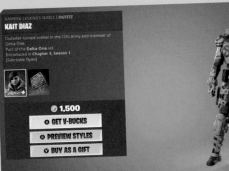

1,500
- GET V-BUCKS
- BUY AS A GIFT

*Marcus has arrived!
Complete a match...
- Gaming or Xbox*

| OUTFIT
ROBOCOP
The future of law enforcement.
Part of the **Omni Consumer Products** set.
Introduced in **Chapter 3, Season 2**.

1,500
- GET V-BUCKS
- BUY AS A GIFT

STAYING SAFE ONLINE

TWO-FACTOR AUTHENTICATION

Two-Factor Authentication (2FA) can be used to help protect your account from unauthorized access by requiring you to enter a security code when you sign in. Check out our how-to video here or help article here.

AUTHENTICATOR APP

Use an Authenticator App as your Two-Factor Authentication (2FA). When you sign in you'll be required to use the security code provided by your Authenticator App.

SMS AUTHENTICATION

Use your phone as your Two-Factor Authentication (2FA) when you sign in you'll be required to use the security code we send you via SMS message.

TWO-FACTOR AUTHENTICATION

You want your account to stay yours, right? Sadly, there are some people out there who gain access to the accounts of others and then either hold them to ransom or steal their skins and V-Bucks. The best way to avoid this is by activating two-factor authentication, or 2FA for short. It simply means you'll have to enter a code from an app or an email address you provide to Epic before you can sign into your account. It keeps your details safe, and you get a free Boogiedown emote. What's not to love?!

PICK AN ANONYMOUS USERNAME

Don't ever have a username that identifies you to the extent that someone could find you by using it. For example, JoeBloggs or JaneDoe where you use your real name as your display name.

BE CAREFUL WHEN ACCEPTING FRIEND REQUESTS

Not everyone on the internet is who they seem to be. If you are sent a friend request by someone you have never spoken to, then treat it with suspicion. You might find you are sent friend requests from people in matches you have played in, but you still shouldn't accept a request from people you don't know. If you're under 18, make sure a parent or guardian knows who is on your friends list and what you are talking about with them.

PLAY SOMEWHERE THAT OTHERS CAN SEE YOU

We all know it's fun to hide away in your room playing Fortnite for hours on end. However, where you can, try and play somewhere that others can see and hear you. It means that if something unpleasant does happen and you are sent an nasty message or similar, others will be able to see it and can help you to deal with it.

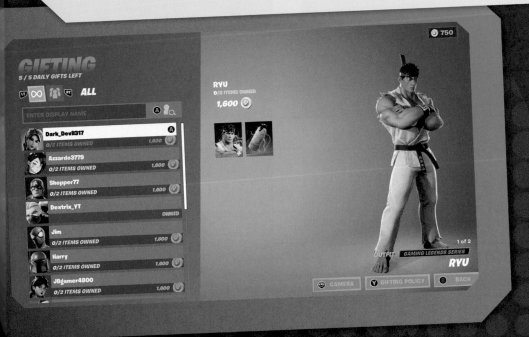

DON'T BE PERSUADED TO BUY GIFTS FOR SOMEONE ELSE

Some players will befriend you, then send you messages asking you to send them gifts. Don't do it. Your V-Bucks belong to YOU. If you want to buy a gift for a genuine friend, then check it is okay with an adult first. If a stranger contacts you demanding you buy them a skin or emote, then tell an adult and block them. It's not appropriate to ask others for gifts unless you know them very well.

IF IT FEELS WRONG, TELL AN ADULT

If anything happens to you online (not just in Fortnite) that doesn't feel right, tell an adult immediately. It might be a parent or guardian, a teacher at school or any other adult that you know and trust. Don't worry that they will think it isn't important – if it feels wrong to you, tell an adult.

DON'T CHAT TO STRANGERS

Keep headphone chat to people you really know – your schoolmates, for example, or relatives. Don't talk to people you don't know, and don't accept messages asking you to do so. You can communicate perfectly well using the in-game emotes, so there's really no need to talk to strangers anyway. Keep your voice chat settings for filled games to party, so that randoms can't join your game and start chatting to you.

QUIZ CORNER!

SO YOU THINK YOU'RE A FORTNITE GURU? TIME TO TEST YOURSELF WITH OUR FIENDISHLY TOUGH PUZZLES!

THE ANSWERS CAN ALL BE FOUND WITHIN THESE VERY PAGES, SO THE CLUES ARE THERE IF YOU ARE STUCK!

ACROSS

4) A name for heals that affect only your shield (5)
6) The name of Midas' chief henchman (6)
7) Explosive weapons that you can throw at your opponents (8)
9) The creators of Fortnite (4)
10) What is said to have happened to a weapon that's been removed from the game (7)
11) The _____ Order, one of the sides in the battle for the Island (8)
12) What AFK is short for (4,4,8)

DOWN

1) The name of the vehicle you start each game on (9)
2) Another word for building yourself into a box while under attack (8)
3) Items that will repair your health to a maximum of 75 (8)
5) A popular mid-range weapon that comes in a variety of different styles (7,5)
8) What you would say about a weapon that has been drastically weakened (6)
12) The weakest of all the building materials (4)

```
I S T O R M T R O O P E R K D
F M S Y E Z Y O P Z K E P I C
E A P H K X E Y K M V I Q S F
S B S O O C H O P P A M T S G
O I J T S T P C C R E A Y H D
F L N O B T G G S V N G P T A
C I A V N A E U U T W I S E B
T T R Z E E L R N Z T N Q A I
S R E E A N S L S X T E U M G
K I D O F R T Y J O K D A R F
I O G E S L B O Y O D O D U O
N S C O Z G I E R H N R S M O
S Z B P H K I E A Y Z D P B T
J O T Z R J G A S M I E J L K
S U L W A T Q W W V I R V E A
```

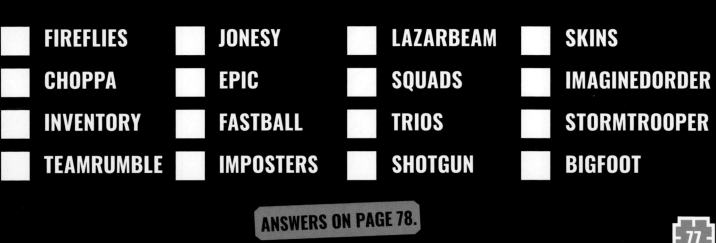

- FIREFLIES
- CHOPPA
- INVENTORY
- TEAMRUMBLE
- JONESY
- EPIC
- FASTBALL
- IMPOSTERS
- LAZARBEAM
- SQUADS
- TRIOS
- SHOTGUN
- SKINS
- IMAGINEDORDER
- STORMTROOPER
- BIGFOOT

ANSWERS ON PAGE 78.

ANSWERS

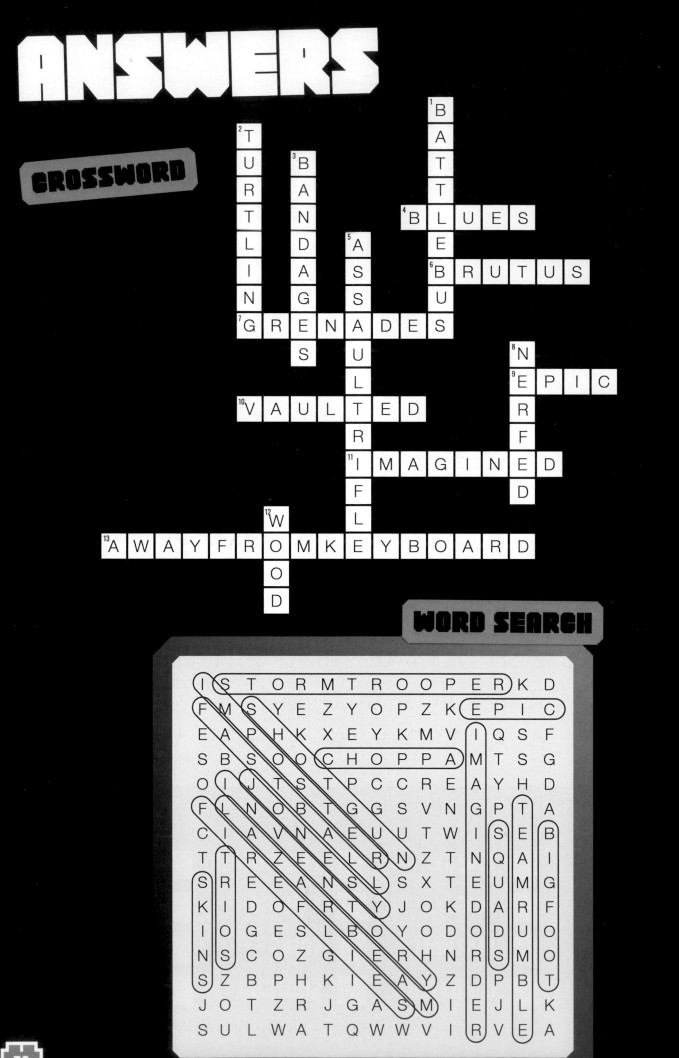

Crossword answers:

1. BATTLEBUS (down)
2. TURTLING (down)
3. BANDAGES (down)
4. BLUES (across)
5. ASSAULTRIFLE (down)
6. BRUTUS (across)
7. GRENADES (across)
8. NERFED (down)
9. EPIC (across)
10. VAULTED (across)
11. IMAGINED (across)
12. WOOD (down)
13. AWAYFROMKEYBOARD (across)

WORD SEARCH

```
I S T O R M T R O O P E R K D
F M S Y E Z Y O P Z K E P I C
E A P H K X E Y K M V I Q S F
S B S O O C H O P P A M T S G
O I J T S T P C C R E A Y H D
F L N O B T G G S V N G P T A
C I A V N A E U U T W I S E B
T T R Z E E L R N Z T N Q T I
S R E E A N S L S X T E U A G
K I D O F R T Y J O K D A R F
I O G E S L B O Y O D O D U O
N S C O Z G I E R H N R S M O
S Z B P H K I E A Y Z D P B T
J O T Z R J G A S M I E J L K
S U L W A T Q W W V I R V E A
```